What Oliver Taught Me

(how my bulldog helped me become a better human)

a memoir

SHERRI GIBBONS

Cover design by Marisa Shor of Cover Me Darling.
Formatted by Marisa Shor of Cover Me Darling and Allyson Gottlieb of Athena
Interior Book Design

In loving memory of Oliver

November 1, 2010 - September 6, 2016

Acknowledgements

Even as a child, I always read the acknowledgment pages of books. I believed if it was important enough for an author to thank these people, I should at least give it the attention it deserves. My hope is you will do the same. Without these people in my life, this book would have never come to fruition. I would have been too busy writing an imaginary book in my head while eating non-imaginary cupcakes.

It goes without saying this book wouldn't have happened if it wasn't for Oliver. Thank you, Oliver, for putting people in our path who were meant to be there. Thank you for inspiring me to write this book. Thank you for all of the lessons you taught me, and for choosing me to be your Mom.

Thank you, thank you, thank you to Jim Gibbons. He is the guy who puts up with my inability to make a decision and stick with it, who puts up with me finding plot holes in every television show and movie we watch, and who tastes every bad recipe I make—even if he has to do so while standing over a garbage can. Thank you for being the best Dad to Winnie and Oliver.

I have eternal gratitude for my parents, Joan and Louis Neno, for always trying to guide me in the right direction even if it seemed I was perilously going in the wrong one. Thank you for all you have done and all you still do.

I have the deepest gratitude for the wisest, kindest, most compassionate woman ever, Lynne Denyer, VMD. You inspired me and validated me while on Oliver's journey, and also on my own.

Thank you for being able to take the emotions and chaos I am feeling inside, and convey them into logical verbalizations. Thank you, a million times over, for being a part of this book and our lives.

So many people have helped me along the way. Some have encouraged me and cheered me on. Some supported me, plugged this book mercilessly on my behalf, or given this non-author some great advice. Some have cried with me or hugged me while I cried. ALL have been amazing friends, and I am so grateful. I need to give special shout outs to the following: Faith Gargan, Rachel Corvasce, and the entire staff at Small Animal Veterinary Associates; Cathy Kittell and the MidAtlantic Bulldog Rescue; Jill Knell; Patty and Tony Vivona; Ronnie Sussman and Doug Buchanan; Taryn Burke; Jennifer Roster; our entire Instagram Bulldog Family; Jan Geisel; the Rathje family; the Alvarez family; Kim, Barbara, and the entire staff of Salty Dog Grooming.

And, to those who left before this book was finished—Patsy Stefanacci and Harry Geisel—you are loved and missed.

Foreword

Chances are if you picked up this book, you have an amazing "fur kid" of your own at home, or somewhere along your life's journey, an animal has changed your life in some remarkable, unforgettable way. Perhaps you've found it difficult to put that understanding into words and into a context that is there for you to guide your life now and into the future. Or, maybe you may have broken the rule that many of us do and were intrigued by Oliver's face on the cover, thinking that the wisdom in those eyes might have something to tell you too about becoming a better human.

As Oliver's primary care veterinarian for all of his life, and as one who has had the great pleasure to learn from so many animals and the people who love them in my twenty-two years of practice, I was honored Sherri asked me to be a part of this memoir. Not long after Sherri had experienced the allergic reaction that could have taken her life, she came into the office with Oliver (a quite regular occurrence) for help. In the over fifteen years or so that I've known and worked with her, I noticed on that day there was something different about her. Sherri, and her bulldogs Winnie and Oliver, shared many parallels in their lives with respect to the many physical challenges that they faced together over many years. Still, no matter how difficult things were with each of them, I never saw Sherri without a smile despite what a bad day it might have been for human or dog, and sometimes both. I could see that Sherri needed to express something. She had told me on more than one occasion during our visits that she'd given serious thought about writing about her life's experiences with Oliver. On that day, I knew this book would be a reality.

Certainly, there isn't any shortage of books available in any media format one chooses if one is interested in growing and evolving in consciousness as a human being. They are written from the point of view of scholars, psychologists, psychiatrists, allopathic and homeopathic physicians, spiritualists, mystics, and gurus to name a few. No matter how lofty or well written, the real value for me in reading these written works on the evolving human is in how easily they can be understood and applied to our own lives in such a way as to live as our authentic, perhaps "higher" selves. Like most bonafide gurus, Oliver taught by example and needed very few words.

In all of the years that I worked with Sherri and Oliver, I watched Sherri grow through the often short-lived victories, and the more difficult and protracted setbacks pertaining to the parallel health challenges that she and Oliver both faced. Remarkably though, whenever Oliver walked into the hospital, no matter how bad a day he might have been having, he greeted everyone in the waiting area with enthusiasm and optimism. His presence was palpable, and everyone felt it. All Sherri could do, at the other end of the leash was smile. That's what we all did. Oliver made you pay attention, and to listen with the heart.

Personally speaking, Oliver challenged me as few others have as a dedicated practitioner of both the art and science of veterinary medicine. Medically speaking, Oliver was nothing short of an enigma. Often having paradoxical reactions to conventional medications, as well as showing remarkable improvements to often simple and unconventional remedies that either Sherri or I would come up with when nothing else seemed to help him. Oliver would just stand there stoically as if wondering what all the worry and fuss was about. Specialists from three different referral hospitals were stymied in their efforts to obtain a definitive diagnosis. Even biopsies of his affected organs, often regarded as the gold standard in any diagnosis, were remarkably inconclusive. In the end, I realized that we were always so busy trying to reason our way through understanding Oliver's medical issues, that we were perhaps missing just enjoying the beauty of his life just as it was in its pure simplicity.

Like Oliver, this book is full of humor (a mark of great wisdom), and as you read along and listen with your own heart, perhaps you may realize what your own animal masters have come into your lives to teach you. In some uncanny way, the universe matched up Sherri with the perfect bulldog to mirror back to her a way to live through her own life and health challenges. With great skills of observation, self-reflection and willingness, Sherri has given us the benefit of her own experience as we all endeavor to be better humans in this world.

Lynne T. Denyer, VMD
Little Egg Harbor, New Jersey

Where It Began

"Holy shit, I think I'm dying!"

For anyone who has ever experienced the severe allergic reaction known as anaphylaxis, you know the above exclamation is an appropriate one. As I sat at a red light on one of the busiest highways in my town with what I knew to be the beginning of anaphylaxis, "Holy shit, I think I'm dying" was not my first (or even tenth) thought. With my eyes glazed over, tears streaming down my face, rivers of snot running out of my nose, and people in cars behind me impatiently honking their horns because traffic was moving but my car wasn't, I didn't think about dying at all. Which is weird, especially for someone who has experienced anaphylaxis before, right? I know how scary that shit is. Hell, I didn't even see my life pass before my eyes the way near-death experiences are typically described. Instead of calling 9-1-1 or thinking about the afterlife, I had one singular thought:

"Who is going to take care of Oliver?"

Before you award me with a Parent of the Year trophy, you need to know that Oliver was not my lovable, mischievous son (because if I had had children, I always pictured my son to be mischievous and most likely, semi-lovable). Oliver wasn't even a ninety-eight-year-old uncle whose adult diapers I had to change and whose sole existence depended on me spooning pureed carrots into his toothless mouth. No, Oliver wasn't either of those. Oliver wasn't even a human being.

Oliver was my not-so-healthy, five-and-a-half-year-old English bulldog.

Go ahead and read that again. I'll give you a second. Done? So, now you know you read that correctly. I wasn't concerned that I was almost in the full throes of anaphylaxis. I wasn't worried that if I called 9-1-1, an ambulance might not make it to me before I gasped my last breath. I wasn't worried that I could die in my car in the middle of traffic in front of a fucking Wawa convenience store. I was worried that my dog might have to hold in his shit a little longer than he's used to holding it. That would probably devastate him, and the fact that he would feel remotely slighted made me a bad "Mom." *That's* what I was thinking about. My dog's fucking *feelings*.

How's that for having my priorities straight? I mean, what the fuck is wrong with me? How could I be so close to possibly dying and not think about my husband, my family, friends, or the milestones in my life? How could I not reflect back on decisions and choices I've made? Why wasn't I wondering if I took the right stances on war and religion and spirituality? Why didn't I think about illnesses and poverty and world peace, or what skin care regimen Rob Lowe uses since he never seems to age? Why wasn't I worried that I could go to Hell because I once ran a scam to help underage kids—myself included—drink at a bar? (It was quite risky and quite involved.) Or even more thought-provoking, why was I more worried about my dog having to take a shit than I was about my life? The short answer: If Oliver had to hold in his shit for a while, that would make me feel guilty because Oliver had an illness that caused him to have diarrhea. He would probably be very upset that he had to do diarrhea and I wasn't around to let him out to the bathroom. Granted, if I had died, I probably wouldn't be capable of actually feeling guilt anymore. But, at the moment while at death's door, I couldn't think too deeply about those things since I was more worried about my dog than my life.

I didn't get into deep contemplation until later that night when I was safe in bed. That's when I began having the appropriate reactions I should have had when I was, you know, actually almost dying. As I stared at the ceiling wide-eyed in the middle of the night with what felt like rigor-mortis because I was so tense. Heart palpitations began, and I started to question my life, my existence, my decisions, choices, causes, actions, reactions—you name it, I thought about it. I. COULD. HAVE. DIED. And had I died, Oliver still would have had to hold in his poop because I'd like to think my husband and family would be too busy identifying my body to be concerned about Oliver and his need to shit.

I couldn't sleep because there were deeper issues rolling around in my brain that kept me awake and had me contemplating every single second of my life. Let's face it, we all make mistakes. And I sure have made a shitload of them. Sometimes, I might make the wrong decision either because I was sabotaging myself or someone else. We all do it; we usually won't admit it. Maybe I spoke harshly. Maybe I lied. Maybe I made poor choices. Maybe I was spiteful. Or resentful. Please don't fucking judge me; if you were honest with yourself, you are more likely than not in the same moral-sinking boat I am. Shit, some of you might already be neck deep in the water. I've done and said stupid things throughout my life. I have let emotions guide my actions and reactions in the worst ways. I allowed people to get under my skin. I have been mean, I have sought revenge. I have not been the best version of myself throughout my life.

I have stuffed feelings down, not spoken up, and have hidden how I felt. More often than I cared to admit, my reactions and actions were guided by gauging how it would impact other people instead of putting myself first. I shied away from living my life to its fullest in case I made someone unhappy along the way. Is this really how I wanted to live? Does life have to be so complicated? Had I died, would I have been happy with who I was as a person? Would I have left a mark in this world? Did I "do the right thing" more often than not? Had I died, would I have been proud of the person I was with the time I was given on this Earth? Truthfully? I wasn't sure. And those thoughts that kept me awake all night led me down a deep rabbit hole which made me wonder: Why do we choose to make our lives so challenging and tumultuous that in the throes of death, we should even have to question ourselves?

Looking back, in the five-and-a-half years since Oliver had chosen us to be his family, I realized that some of the most pivotal, critical, tragic, troublesome, and future-affecting things have occurred to me in that span of time. Sure, our entire lives are filled with ups and downs, but some big life decisions and situations have happened in the past five years, more than any other time in my life. I also realized I could have handled every single one of those decisions and situations differently—or at the very least, viewed them differently and reacted better.

Reflecting on this all night long and into the next day, when three mugs of coffee still couldn't shake away my thoughts, I had an epiphany of sorts: Why do we make life so difficult for ourselves and those around us? It doesn't have to be this way. Why are we not living authentically? Why do we let our fears of disappointing someone else guide us? Why do we impose our insecurities onto other people? Why do we feel the fear of failure instead of the excitement of what could be if we would only try? We, as human beings, make living difficult. We live our lives in such a way that our emotions overlap; we take other people's issues on as our own. We are walking billboards of insecurity. Why do we not make decisions for ourselves, but instead, base our decisions on how others will perceive us? Why couldn't we live with simple thoughts, actions, reactions, enjoyment, understanding, positivity, compassion, and pure love? You know, sort of like how a dog lives. *Like Oliver.*

I spent the following day alternating between staring at Oliver and watching him spend his day in sweet, blissful contentment, asking myself, "Why am I not living like Oliver?" And listen, I get it. As humans, there are complexities that are unavoidable. I mean, who wouldn't love to lie around all day and get attention and have our butts wiped for us? I'm not stupid; I know dogs operate in a more simplistic way fundamentally. Still, why couldn't we take some of that purity and apply it to our lives? Even just the smallest amount of simplicity could better our lives, right?

I asked myself that question over and over before realizing, this little curmudgeon of a dog had given me gentler reminders of how to be a better human. I just didn't know it until this near-death moment caused me to look deeper into my life and how almost every scary, tumultuous, weird, or sad situation I had been in was paralleling Oliver's life. He has given me clues and had I only looked to him in the thick of stressful circumstances and decisions; I could have lived a more authentic life. Oliver was super happy to have a roof over his head, food in his belly, and a warm place to sleep. Butt scratches, playing with friends, and chowing down on treats were all just bonuses. Life is so simple if you strip away as much of the bullshit as you can. Oliver didn't have any bullshit in his life at all. I realized I could be a better human if I would just open up my eyes and take some cues from Oliver.

So, this is where it all began. This near-death experience was the moment when I looked back at some critical moments in my life. It was the moment in my life where, if I were a cartoon, you would have seen a lightbulb appear brightly illuminated above my noggin. This was the catalyst that helped me realize I could have made better decisions, behaved and reacted differently had I opened my eyes and lived life like Oliver.

This isn't a midlife crisis; this is a midlife awakening. This is the story of a neurotic, weird chick who always has complicated her life until she almost died and realized life would be so much better if she lived it like her quirky, funny bulldog, Oliver. This is the story of looking back at pivotal moments and realizing the lessons that needed to be learned were right in front of my eyes, coming to me via my oddball bulldog. I learned a lot of those lessons in the thick of situations; some I am still learning. This is the story of how my bulldog helped me become a better human, and how I finally woke up and realized it.

chapter ONE

After one year of marriage and living in a crappy one-bedroom apartment in a sketchy building in Highland Park, New Jersey, my husband Jimmy and I bought a house in our hometown of Toms River. Three months after moving into our new home we decided we should buy a puppy. An English bulldog puppy. Why an English bulldog? Because we fell for the stereotype of bulldogs being low maintenance and lazy. And so we did what most people do: without research or any experience whatsoever, we called the closest pet store and plunked $1,800 down on our very first kid with fur. We didn't know much about bulldogs or dogs in general, except that they need food and most likely would enjoy some water, too. Winnie was a beautiful white and fawn English bulldog, and if our first interaction with her was indicative of what life with her would be like, we should have immediately turned around and walked out of the pet store. As soon as she came out of her "holding area" she ran around uncontrollably, dodging people and free-standing product displays, wouldn't listen to anyone and then promptly squatted and took a shit in the corner of the store. Oh yeah, we were in for it.

Despite the pet store giving us her "papers" that said she was purebred, you could tell by looking at her that her brother's nephew's uncle was most likely her father—if you catch my subtle drift. Sadly, puppy mills weren't discussed way back in the dinosaur age of 1998. The general public didn't know much about them and wouldn't know much about them until many years later. An enormous red flag was that she was shipped from a farm out-of-state. Of course, there are breeders everywhere but selling to a pet store most likely isn't their plan if they are reputable. These were things we didn't know back then, and despite realizing a few years later that Winnie was more than likely from a puppy mill, we are still forever grateful she came into our lives.

Within five minutes of meeting Winnie, a couple of things were clear. Firstly, we loved her and would be taking her home. Secondly, she was not the stereotypical lazy bulldog that we expected. She was high-strung, even for a puppy. In fact, as time went by and we learned more about puppy mills, we realized Winnie was taken away from her mother too soon and probably never experienced a waking moment outside of a crate, cage, or holding area in the six weeks of her life before us taking her home.

After an initial examination with a random vet—whom I had only known because the family dog I had as a child had gone to her—we learned Winnie had hip dysplasia, closed tear ducts, and a few other minor problems. The veterinarian who examined her relayed to us exactly what hip dysplasia was and how serious it could be. She suggested we take her back to the pet store based on the hip dysplasia diagnosis alone and demand a refund. She then proceeded to tell us if we did do that, Winnie would most likely be euthanized. And so we did what any normal people would do: we ignored the vet, spent a lot of money on a puppy who had a bunch of (mostly) external medical conditions, crossed our fingers and hoped for the best. Over the years, allergies, seasonal Alopecia, along with several other ailments, materialized. If there is a medical condition you could think of, Winnie probably had it. Thankfully, most were minor things: eye infections, ear infections, pulled muscles, food allergies, skin allergies and colitis all made appearances over Winnie's life. We did all we could to make sure Winnie's medical issues were always under control. Was it costly? YES. Was it sometimes worrisome? YES. Was it worth it? YES, YES, YES! We considered ourselves very lucky, however, after hearing more and more horror stories as pet stores became more well known as puppy mill havens. We eventually changed veterinarians and are so thankful we did. Through the care of our amazingly compassionate and knowledgeable new veterinarian, Lynne Denyer, Winnie lived a mostly healthy (read: spoiled) life. There wasn't one ailment that bothered or disabled the Winnister, including her hip dysplasia. Her medical issues never changed how cute she was and how in love with her we fell. Nor did they affect her quality of life. She ran, jumped, and hopped around without any limitations.

If those first few paragraphs didn't make it clear, let me lay it all out for you. English bulldogs are the Ferraris of the dog world. They are high maintenance and require tons of time and money just to keep them running. They are everything we never thought they were. They are not low-maintenance. There should be a book titled, *So You Want an English Bulldog? You Might As Well Open Your Window and Throw Hundred Dollar Bills Out of It!* (In fact, maybe that will be the title of my next book.)

Still, Winnie was a sweet puppy and grew into a very loving dog. The fact that most of her adult teeth never grew in didn't bother her nearly as much as it bothered me. I figured it would be good practice for when I would most assuredly have to spoon-feed Jimmy when he was old and toothless. (Jimmy is forty-seven years old and has only one cavity. It's bound to catch up with him some time, isn't it?) Sure, sometimes food fell out of Winnie's mouth, and her Alopecia left her with huge bald patches in various areas of her body, but she never let that get her down. She chomped ice cubes with her gums and allowed me to put a scarf and coat over her bald spots in the winter.

Winnie didn't have any rules. Not because she didn't want them but because we were too stupid to set them. We now know that is wrong, but in the thick of it, we thought it was super cute that every time a motorcycle would drive down our street, Winnie would run along the back of our couch causing it irreparable damage. She slept in our bed with us, ate "people food," climbed all over our furniture and OWNED us. I used to half-joke that I would most likely end up needing a wheelchair by the time I hit the age of forty because of constantly having to sleep in the fetal position as Winnie sprawled her large bulldog body comfortably across the bed.

Most bulldog owners will tell you bulldogs are, uh, unique. They are very quirky and do strange things, and Winnie wasn't any exception. She would be sweetly lying down on her bed then suddenly stand up and begin running through the entire house as though it was her personal race track. Winnie would look like she was in some weird trance and blinded by something she could only see in her mind, something that caused her to run as fast as she could, banging into furniture as she went. She also felt the need to hump Jimmy every time she pooped. It never failed. Any time my father walked into the house, she ran to her bowl and began to eat as though it was her last meal. *Every time.* She couldn't walk by any mailbox without trying to attack it. She had a favorite stuffed frog that she suckled like a baby would a pacifier, yet she might rip its arms off at any given time and then cry in front of the garbage can after I threw it away. I began buying them in bulk because if she was without "Froggy," she was depressed.

The oddest thing, however, about Winnie was she could talk. No shit! In fact, *America's Funniest Home Videos* featured Winnie as "The I Love You Bulldog" because she said, "I love you." Before you close this book while shaking your head and muttering to yourself, "This bitch is crazy," trust me, I understand she wasn't talking. But it was human-sounding enough to get her on TV, and that's probably more than your dog has ever done, so that's pretty impressive. That video has circled the globe as part of many other bulldog compilation videos. It's always startling to click a link thinking I am going to see a bunch of weird bulldogs doing crazy things—and then Winnie pops up in it. Even now, six years since Winnie has passed away, I will still get phone calls when a rerun of her episode of *America's Funniest Home Videos* airs.

From the time we brought Winnie into our lives in 1998 until 2005, Jimmy and I both worked full-time. I worked many, many hours as a retail manager but was close enough to home where if I needed to, I could run home on lunch or dinner breaks to take care of Winnie. In 2005, gastrointestinal issues that I had faced and ignored for years became worse. I wasn't sure what was wrong with me, and I wasn't even sure I wanted to know. As I became sicker in 2005, and ultimately left my career behind to put my health first while doctors tried to determine what was wrong with me, Winnie stuck by my side. When I was finally properly diagnosed with severe Crohn's disease in 2006, Winnie was who I turned to for comfort while Jimmy was at work. Sure, she didn't know what was wrong with me, but she understood I wasn't feeling well. We developed a nice routine of several short walks per day, followed by her favorite thing: several car rides per day. Winnie loved standing on the backseat and watching the neighborhood whizz by outside. Those short walks and rides in the car not only allowed me brief escapes from the psychological warfare regarding what living with an incurable illness would be like, but it also tired the shit out of Winnie. Score!

Knowing the life expectancy for bulldogs wasn't typically very long compared to other breeds, I began to have constant stress and fear regarding her death as Winnie grew older. My biggest concern would be Winnie passing away at home. I wouldn't know what to do, or how to handle it. As time went on, you could see telltale signs of

Winnie's age. Seeing her physical body shrink was unavoidable. She took longer naps and was always in a deep sleep. I would often walk into a room to find her sleeping, and I would pause and watch her intently to make sure she was breathing. It was slowly driving me insane. There are times now when I think back and realize I spent way too much time waiting for Winnie to die instead of focusing on her being alive. I feel we, as humans, do that often with people, too. Whether a family member is old, or whether they have been diagnosed with a terminal illness, at some point throughout humanity, we began to expect the future before learning to enjoy the present. Sadly, this lesson is usually learned too late.

In 2010, I became very sick, and I was admitted to the hospital. The tests and X-rays and ultrasounds showed I was inflamed from my esophagus all the way through my colon. I was in extreme pain and was placed into isolation until doctors could be sure this was Crohn's flaring up and not Clostridium Difficile, also known as C.Diff. Since Jimmy was juggling work along with me being in the hospital, my parents were able to help with Winnie by going over to our house to feed her and let her out to the bathroom. My father reported back to me each time and would say he felt as though Winnie missed me because she wasn't acting like herself when she saw him. Jimmy would say the same; she just wasn't herself. We all chalked it up to her being confused at my sudden disappearance for seven days.

When my doctor finally released me from the hospital, I couldn't wait to get home to my Winnie Magoo. When I walked in the house after being gone for seven days, I couldn't believe how little she looked. When you are with someone—two-legged or four-legged—every waking minute, you don't see the subtle changes in them. It was only after having been away in the hospital for a week that I was able to come home and see what everyone else saw. Winnie was old. She was a senior. Our time was fleeting. I began a new obsessive-compulsive routine of telling Winnie every morning and every night,

"Winnie, we never want you to suffer or be in pain. Please, please, please, if you are ever sick, find a way to let us know."

One short month later, in October of 2010 and at the age of twelve-and-a-half, Winnie began acting strangely. After some x-rays of her stomach had shown she had eaten a large rock, we were so perplexed as to how, where, when, and why she swallowed a rock. Winnie never went anywhere we weren't. One of us always supervised her when she was in the backyard, and we didn't even have rocks like that anywhere. We were confused. Dr. Denyer advised us to wait a few days to see if Winnie would pass the rock on her own. When that didn't happen, we went to NorthStar Vets, a hospital not too far away from us. The next step was to have an endoscopy performed to see if the doctor could remove the rock in that manner. Unfortunately, we never made it that far.

On the day of Winnie's endoscopy, I was at the hospital, hooked up to an IV receiving my infusion for Crohn's disease, so Jimmy was flying solo at the veterinary hospital. He brought Winnie for her endoscopy and met with an excellent internist, Dr. Tammy Anderson, who was going to perform the endoscopy after Winnie had some pre-admission testing. The x-rays showed something we weren't expecting: cancer. We never had an inkling; she never acted out-of-sorts, aside from swallowing a rock. The endoscopy wasn't performed, and Jimmy had the difficult task of telling me our precious first fur-baby had cancer when I came home from my treatment.

The day the cancer was found was the day we let Winnie go. The ten-minute drive to our veterinarian's office was the longest drive in the world, filled with tears and tears and more tears. Dr. Denyer and her staff treated Winnie with so much love and respect from the moment they first met her, right up until her final breath. My heart was shattered. Jimmy and I held her while she sank into a deep and final slumber. I was devastated. The pain we felt was horrendous, and I never wanted to experience it ever again. It was not an easy decision to let her go, and sure, a lot of people might say, "Jeez, she was twelve-and-a-half! She lived a full life!" Oh, how I want to punch those people in their throats! It doesn't matter how old a pet is; when it is time to let them go, it is heartbreaking and gut-wrenching, whether they only had a few years, or whether it was twelve years. (Seriously, why do parrots and turtles live a hundred years and dogs a lot less? Can we fix that?) Winnie loved us, and we loved her. We took care of her, and in her doggish way, she took care of us, especially me as I navigated my Crohn's diagnosis, being unable to work, and everything that fell in between. Jimmy and I were always in agreement that we would never let Winnie suffer. I become a crazed lunatic when I know of people who keep their pets alive simply because it is too difficult of a decision to let them go. Our pets give us true unconditional love. To keep them alive when they are suffering is selfish and not okay in my opinion. Still, even with sickness, making THE decision is hard.

I realized, driving home without our Winnie, that she swallowed that rock to set in motion a way for us to find her cancer. I know, I know. You probably think that is a stretch, but I believe nothing in this world is coincidental. It can't be. And I begged her to find a way to let us know if she was ever sick. That rock was how she did it. We will never know where that rock came from or when she swallowed it—but I will always be grateful it set in motion a way for Winnie to let us know it was time to set her free.

That first night without Winnie was unbearable. As soon as we came home from the vet's office, we began systematically throwing away any of her things we couldn't donate. It was a way to stay busy and not think about her being gone. As I threw out her crusty, smelly bones, I begged her for a sign. I needed her to let me know she was now safe and pain-free. For those who know me, I am a big believer in signs. I feel we sometimes need signs in our lives to keep us going, or remind us of where we need to be. Or, in this case, to comfort us.

My sign came two days later. It was a Sunday, and Jimmy had the day off from work. We were both in the thickness of grief and knew we needed to get out of the house. We decided to take a ride to the boardwalk in Point Pleasant, just a short fifteen minutes away, but a place we never, ever visit. We walked up to the boardwalk after parking our car and two steps into our walk there was a white concrete bench that had "Winnie" painted in black on the side with a big red heart next to it. These benches lined the boardwalk and residents could pay to have names painted onto them. We will never know who that bench was in honor of, but the odds of us choosing that section of the boardwalk on that day was a clear sign for me. And in case we weren't one hundred percent sure *that* sign was meant for us, when we returned home from our walk, our entire house smelled like one giant Winnie fart. And her farts were fierce. If you've ever smelled a bulldog fart, you will know there isn't anything in the world that can quite replicate the stench. She had given me my signs. She was okay and happily farting away in Heaven.

Winnie was such a great dog despite her ailments, and she filled our house with so much life that after losing her, our house was depressingly empty. Being unable to work due to Crohn's, Winnie was my partner-in-crime, and we spent every day together. She saw me through the highs and lows (okay, mostly lows) as I navigated being diagnosed with an incurable illness and the impact it was having on my life. Spending hours alone at home while Crohn's crushed my physical and mental wellbeing was made a lot easier with Winnie by my side. She would cuddle up next to me on our bed when I was sick, or squeeze herself onto the couch next to me as each medication the doctors tried made me feel even worse. She was my ride-or-die bitch. I would speak to her all day long. She was my shadow and followed me everywhere I went. It wasn't unusual for her to use her noggin to barge into the bathroom. There wasn't any door in our house that could keep Winnie out of any room. She would ram her giant bulldog head into it until it opened. After she died, I would cry hysterically while alone in the house and yell out, "WINNIE CAN YOU STILL HEAR ME?" I felt so lonely, and I didn't know how to be alone. Jimmy had a small reprieve by going to work for eight hours a day, but my days were, well, quiet. Taking care of a fur kid for twelve years and then suddenly not having her here anymore left a gaping hole that didn't ever seem like it could be filled again.

Jimmy and I agreed we wanted another bulldog and felt that a six-month mourning period would be appropriate. We fell in love with the breed, and despite their medical issues, we knew we would always be "bully parents." I was hopeful that in those six months, a robotic dog that never died would be invented. It wasn't. We didn't want to rush out and "replace" Winnie; she was irreplaceable. We lasted one month after her passing before the house was too empty to tolerate. We vowed this time would be different. We'd research more! We'd watch the *Dog Whisperer*! We'd read books on training! We wouldn't let the dog on our furniture or sleep in our bed! It wouldn't be allowed to eat "people food!" We'd Google the shit out of all things bulldog! We were going to be the BEST bulldog owners on this freaking planet!

And we did do those things. *Mostly.*

Since I had the freest time, I began researching rescues and filled out an application for a successful local bulldog rescue. They asked for a donation, so I made one. We were never contacted by them again, nor did they respond to me when I reached out to them multiple times to inquire about our application. And while this upset me greatly, I know they are doing good things for bulldogs; it just wasn't meant to be with that particular rescue. At that time, bulldogs weren't as popular as they are now and the chances were slim to adopt one from this rescue, anyway. And so, we switched gears.

By this time puppy mills were being discussed more, and we knew then what we didn't find out when we brought Winnie home, so we knew going to a pet store was out of the equation. We felt we wanted to make right choices and felt finding a reputable breeder was the best way to bring another bulldog into our family. I started by doing basic web searches and visiting different breeders' websites. I found a breeder in a town about thirty minutes away, and I emailed him. While I didn't think we were immediately ready for a puppy, I felt it was important to make contact and learn as much as I could from breeders. He was quick to respond to me and sent me a photo of a bulldog puppy that was gorgeous. I explained to him we weren't ready, having just lost Winnie a month prior. He asked for our phone number and explained he'd like to speak to me rather than email.

He called me and began putting some pressure on me by tugging at my heartstrings. "This puppy is so perfect, and I know you will love her! She is gorgeous, she is purebred, and she is going to go fast if you don't take her!" He explained that he typically had a waiting list for his puppies, but he was moved by my emails discussing Winnie and felt that we would be great bulldog parents. I listened to him and fell for it all. I explained I needed to speak with my husband and I did. He wanted $3,000 for this puppy. This was a big decision for us.

Jimmy and I discussed it and stared at the photos of this beautiful girl. We decided we would go for it, but of course, wanted to visit her first and interact with her, as well as get more information regarding his breeding practice. I explained that to him on the first of many voicemails. We went through a weird pattern of sorts where I would call the breeder and he wouldn't return my call but instead would reply to it via email. It was a never-ending game of phone and email tag. It was frustrating. Bringing a new puppy into our lives was a big decision for us, and it started to feel like something was wrong with this breeder, and everything was SCREAMING "red flag," but it was too late. We had seen the pictures of the puppy and were already deciding on a name! Finally, this breeder made a critical error. He called me by mistake and left a voicemail, but the voicemail was for someone else, offering them the same puppy for $3,500! He was trying to sell the puppy, *our puppy*, to the highest bidder. It was sickening to me and left me feeling so disheartened.

The emotional high of planning to bring a new puppy home after losing Winnie, to the depression of finding out this breeder was essentially running a scam, was awful. It felt so shitty to realize this puppy—whose picture I had been staring at for a couple of weeks—wasn't going to be our puppy. That crappy feeling lasted a couple of days, and then I became furious. And after speaking to many other people, I found out these types of scams are common, especially with bulldog breeds. Since bulldogs were now gaining in popularity, people were willing to pay a lot of money for them. That breeder never realized he called the wrong house and we moved on. I left him one message letting him know he was "caught" but never heard from him again. We realized we needed to be much more careful. Everything happens the way it is supposed to happen, even if it isn't pleasant or what we would necessarily want. There was a reason we didn't end up with that puppy. Perhaps some higher power was guiding us in a direction that was different from the one in which we were heading. And so, the search was back on.

Through the Bulldog Club of America, we were able to find a reputable breeder—a husband and wife team who lived about an hour and a half away from our home. After reading every single word on their website, I reached out via email to Patti and Michael Rathje. I didn't ask if they had any puppies. I asked questions about the breeding practices they used and explained how we were recently burned by a breeder. I then went on to detail Winnie's life, and what life had been like since losing her. We began a series of emails getting to know each other, learning about the health of their dogs, and the genetic testing they did. They explained to us they competed in dog shows and the health of their dogs is critical to their success. Michael replied to one of my emails saying how refreshing it was that my first two questions to them weren't, "Do you have any puppies? How much are they?" In fact, it was weeks before we even knew they had three puppies available. They invited us to their home to meet them and their puppies, as well as the litter's mother and father. There was never any pressure from them, and they encouraged us to ask as many questions as we needed to ask them.

As we drove to the Rathje's house, I had this weird feeling of excitement mixed with guilt. Was this okay? Was it too soon? Would Winnie be upset we were considering a new dog? Maybe the botched experience with the first breeder was a sign not to get another dog just yet? Did we take enough time to honor Winnie's life? I kept picturing Winnie looking down at us shaking her toothless head in sadness because we were "over" her so quickly. I'd say huge, sloppy tears were running out of her eyes as she looked down at us, but because she had closed tear ducts, that was one less unnerving and sad vision my mind could bypass. The conflict between wanting a new puppy while still mourning Winnie was sickening, especially when I was still crying daily over losing her. Seriously, though, anyone who has ever seen an English bulldog puppy can attest that you will instantly want to scoop it up and eat its face off because they are that adorable. I knew where this was heading even if my soul was wrestling with it.

We met with Patti and Michael and visited with the three puppies they had. All were from the same litter—two males, and a female. All three puppies instantly began gnawing on my fingers and were so utterly adorable. We were even able to visit with the mother and father of the litter, each equally healthy, great looking—and fat. The female puppy was all white, just like their mother, with the cutest brindle patch on her butt. One male was fawn and white with brown rings around both eyes and looked very much like their father. The other male was the one puppy they had available, and he was a perfect combination of both mother and father. He had a huge, white head with cute speckled ears and the cutest fawn and white body. The left side of his face sported white eyelashes while the right side featured black lashes and a funny, vertical black line that made it look as though he had one eyebrow which made him look permanently grumpy on only one side of his face. He was gorgeous and rambunctious, and I was able to check off so many things Google told me to look for in a bulldog puppy, such as a nice straight back, wide nostrils, a tail that wasn't corkscrew and a few other superficial details. On his back, close to his cute puppy butt, was a tiny stroke of white as though someone came along a spilled a little paint onto his brown ass. He was the cutest thing, ever.

As this bundle of puppy goodness tried to bite off my face, fingers, and ankles, I instantly knew he would be our new fur kid. This was it: I had to reconcile the guilt I felt about moving on from Winnie with the happiness I felt holding this puppy. I didn't love Winnie any less now that she was gone. I simply had enough love to give to another dog, too. I wasn't going to forget about Winnie and our lives together. I was merely making some room for some new puppy love. Right? Our decision was made! This puppy was going to be ours! He was healthy! He was purebred! He was going to be a walking example of what a healthy bulldog should be! People will stop us in the street and say, "What a perfect, healthy, well-trained bulldog you have there!"

Unfortunately, he was still too young to come home with us. As we waited a few more weeks, I would often stifle the little twinge of guilt that would creep around at the back of my brain. And that guilt grew and grew until it turned into a full-fledged raised-in-a-Catholic-church mountain of GUILT. Thanks, brain. The inner dialogue in my head was relentless. "Would Winnie be upset if we get a new puppy? Will she think we don't love her anymore even though I talk to her ashes every time I walk past the box they are kept in and tell her I love and miss her? Will she think she is being replaced? Can ghost dogs even think? Am I weird?" I was so overwhelmed by the guilt of replacing the dog I was still grieving, I almost backed out of getting this new, cute, little puppy. I had many conversations with Jimmy about it and honestly felt as though my heart was exploding from guilt. Still, there was something about this puppy. He looked directly into my eyes when we met as if to say, "I'm choosing YOU. You will be my weird dog Mom, and we will have some adventures!" The Ghost of Winnie would have to understand. We wanted that puppy. He chose us; how could we not make him a member of our family and our second fur kid? I mean, HE. LOOKED. INTO. MY. EYES.

Why was I allowing my weird guilt to dampen our excitement for this new time in our lives? Why couldn't I love and honor Winnie while loving this beautiful, little bundle of puppy goodness? Why do we do that—why do we allow guilt to shut down our joy? It wasn't about grieving Winnie; I felt like a horrible person for being happy about this new puppy so soon after the sadness of life without Winnie. I sensed it; this puppy loved me from the moment we locked eyes. It was a joy that I needed to allow myself to feel. And I needed to convince myself it was okay to feel that joy.

On January 16, 2011, at the age of eleven weeks old, he came home with us. We named him Oliver, and he lit up our world with love, sweetness, craziness, laughter and lots of poop.

What Oliver Taught Me: Oliver was destined to be with us and the failed attempts in contacting rescues and other breeders, while disappointing, were supposed to happen because Oliver wanted us. I needed Oliver, and so he was put into my life. I had things I needed to learn and be reminded of, and Oliver was the one who planned on doing the job. Each time I would cry over losing Winnie after Oliver joined our family, he would stare up at me, nudge my leg a little. It was his way of letting me know it was okay to grieve Winnie. There isn't a time limit on grieving, even for a pet. Oliver showed me; it is normal to allow a crack of light to shine through your cold, dead, grieving heart. In fact, you should. It is healing. Trust and believe that life unfolds the way it is intended to and even if it isn't apparent at the moment, it will be fine. Life will be as it is supposed to be.

chapter
TWO

The first few days of having a dog again—much less a puppy—back in the house were hectic and weird. But nice. Oliver was very curious and seemed pretty smart. Unfortunately, when we brought him home on that cold day in January 2011, we had just been hit with a blizzard. Jimmy and I prepared for Oliver. We read books, watched videos and promised each other we would be in control. As much as we loved Winnie, we certainly could recognize that letting her eat "people food," jump all over our furniture and sleep in bed with us was not the route we were going to take with Oliver. We set a precedent immediately by holding onto his leash and making him wait as we stepped into the front door first. According to our research, this is supposed to establish that we are the "masters of the domain." I'm not sure if Oliver knew or cared who was in charge at that moment; he was tired from a long car ride and wanted to hurry up, get inside and explore. And explore he did! After running like a lunatic through the entire house, our little furball ran into his crate that was set up with padding, a comfy blanket and some stuffed toys. It must have met his expectations because he came back out and then promptly took a shit under the dining room table.

Have you ever tried house training a puppy in two feet of snow? It was a nightmare. First, we needed to buy a circular fence so we could keep Oliver contained in a particular area. Second, we needed to remove that huge, round area of two feet of snow. Oliver was petrified of the snow and even the grass, as he had never had stepped on either before. Thankfully, he caught on quickly and realized that being put down in the grass and snow doesn't mean you are supposed to eat the grass and snow, but rather, relieve yourself on it.

He was the cutest thing ever as he followed me all around the house like a duckling would follow its mother. He explored the house but was so fond of his crate that we knew we made the correct choice in crate training him, something we never did with Winnie. Jimmy and I were so proud of how mellow and sweet he was as he climbed with his almost-too-big-paws up into my lap. He would sleep through the night in his crate, and when I would wake up in the morning, and he would see me, his ears would pull back, and he could not contain his wiggle and excitement. It was so pleasant to go from checking to see if our twelve-year-old bulldog, Winnie, was still breathing, to seeing so much excitement and life in Oliver. He let me kiss him and cuddle him, and I was in Heaven. Oliver loved meeting our families and friends and was so mellow; everyone couldn't believe how amazingly sweet this little guy was! It was all sunshine and lollipops and ice cream and unicorns.

Yeah, that lasted for about forty-eight hours. Then Oliver became some weird kind of demonic terrorist. It was as though some remote timer in another dimension was set to go off exactly two days after bringing Oliver home. We referred to it in hushed tones as the Timer O' Terror. It was as if his cute, sweet demeanor was some ploy to get us to love him and bring him home and now that we did, he was going to take over the Earth using his super-power of Evilness.

There were a few times in my life where I wondered if I made the right decision of not having kids. A week into Oliver coming home with us solidified I made the correct choice. If I somehow ended up with a human child who behaved even half as badly as Demon Spawn Oliver, you would have seen me on the nightly news for abandoning the kid in a parking lot. Oliver, seemingly overnight, became the Devil incarnate. He turned into a fucking shark disguised as a cute puppy. The little shit drew blood from one of my body parts every fifteen minutes. He ripped pants, hoodies, sneakers and flesh. He let out his first tiny bark when he was reprimanded with the word, "No!" It was his way of saying, "Fuck you" to us. He slept with his right eye open which added in a creep-factor to his demonic behavior in a big way. The first time I saw it, I thought he was dead. Like, *literally* dead. I started to feel as though I might vomit and became hot and weird and upset. Then I heard him snore. Sleeping with that right eye open, it was as though he was never truly resting, but instead, he was watching and waiting to assassinate us.

He was a walking, barking, biting nightmare. He began trying to hump Jimmy to establish dominance and reprimanding this furry psycho meant putting your life at risk. We put all of our research into action and tried the "Shhh" method. When Oliver would begin any undesirable behavior, we would summon up our inner *Dog Whisperer* and say, "Shhh!" While Caesar Milan's dogs instantly obeyed his "shhhs," Oliver was riled up by ours. He would lunge at anyone who dared to "shhh" him. While I took the brunt of his biting since Jimmy was at work all day, I knew I had to find something— anything—to stop Oliver in his tracks. The next tactic I tried was pretending to be hurt and give a small whimper, turning my back on Oliver any time he bit me. All that did was put me in a vulnerable position as Oliver realized he could simply attack and bite the back of me. Nothing worked. And teething? Jesus, the teething was the worst. He was ornery and mean and nasty and, well, bitey. The fact that he was gaining almost two pounds per week also struck fear into my soul. Not only was our puppy a teething psychopath, but he was going to be a giant, fat, teething psychopath.

What I didn't think about thoroughly before taking on living with a puppy was the effect it would have on my Crohn's disease. By the time I had finally been diagnosed in 2006, Winnie was already the ripe old age of eight and didn't require the amount of care a puppy needed. For each time Oliver stepped in his poop, there were roughly four times that amount of trips running to the bathroom with severe diarrhea for me. Despite starting Remicade infusions in 2007 and trying many other drugs before that, I never achieved a remission. While I didn't even know what *my* normal was anymore, I did know stress made things even worse and living with this satanic puppy was stressful. The mere fact that Oliver didn't want to listen or learn caused even more stress, which in turn, caused my Crohn's to become even worse.

Before Oliver, I had already accepted living half of a life. Medication after medication failed me. Why weren't any drugs—the drugs that majority of Crohn's patients have success with—helping me? I wanted to give up on my wonderful, compassionate and caring doctor because he was at a loss for what to do to help me and I believe there were just as many times that he would have been happy to see me find another doctor. His frustration with my lack of response to medication was just as intense as mine. He told me more than once I was a "challenging case" yet we stuck together. We discussed my symptoms in-depth at each visit. Knowing I always need a "safety net" of sorts, he always made sure another drug was lined up on the horizon when the drug of the moment didn't work in its allotted time. While I appreciated and was grateful for his perseverance, there were days when I wanted to stop all medications and just let things get so bad that I would have to have some of my intestines cut out. Maybe then I'd find some relief.

I began to accept that Crohn's disease was my life and I was letting it define me. I felt alone in my struggle because I couldn't even accurately describe how I felt and I also have a weird hang-up of feeling guilty for telling people I am in pain. A mantra I developed over the years was, "There is always someone who has it worse so don't complain, you asshole." And honestly, that is a shitty way to think. Of course, there will always be someone in a worse place than we are; that doesn't mean what we are going through isn't any less painful or shitty. We shouldn't diminish our experiences and brush off emotions that are so relevant as part of our healing. Feeling depressed because I have Crohn's and sad because the medication wasn't working to help me is a part of my life, my reality. I needed to learn my feelings were valid. I was at a point in my illness where I simply had to trust I would eventually get to a place where I would feel better. Still, not finding relief sucks. Not finding a medication to force a remission sucks even more. And feeling alone in your illness sucks the most. And whatever the situation is in your life—illness, divorce, unemployment, whatever it is—it is okay to say that it sucks.

When your illness prevents you from traveling, eating out at restaurants, sitting through a movie, or even just comfortably hanging out with friends, you stop doing those things. The longer you go without doing those things, people forget you exist. A dog always knows you're there because you are the one cleaning the crap from its butt when it can't quite pinch it off. Maybe that is why having a furry companion has always meant so much to me. Winnie—and now Oliver—never once judged me for my inability to do certain things the way my human friends did. When you cancel plans constantly with people, they stop making plans with you. They stop calling you. I don't believe that anyone who has never had a chronic illness can comprehend the loneliness that comes along with having one. As someone who avoids confrontation, I could never jump up and down, wave my hands and scream, "HEY GUYS! I'M STILL HERE! DON'T FORGET ABOUT ME!" So how did I handle the sadness of losing friends over the years? I didn't. I ignored those feelings and now instead of even thinking about it, I focused on my weird, demonic puppy.

As a few weeks passed, nothing changed except my Crohn's symptoms worsened, I heard less from friends, and Oliver just became bigger and fatter. And meaner. As he gained even more weight, I swear each of those pounds gave him super-canine strength. Oddly, what he gained in strength, he lost in brain power. He was vicious and dumb all at the same time. I didn't even know that was possible; I assumed you needed to be smart to plot mass destruction and evilness. He was a fur-covered horror show of a puppy with the brain of Gomer Pyle. A typical morning with Oliver would consist of him ripping the flesh from one or ten of my fingers and snarling like a rabid wolf one minute, and then freaking out and whimpering when seeing his shadow on the floor. He would drop a load of poop and then step in it. He would look at me straight in my eyes and STEP. IN. HIS. OWN. SHIT. More than once!!! And I swear he was laughing at me while I cleaned the squishy, smelly crap from between his gigantic toes. He would tear apart a cuddly, stuffed animal in three seconds flat and then run underneath coffee table and smash his head into it. *Repeatedly.* Now that I give it some thought, maybe he got dumber *because* he was smashing his head so often into the coffee table. Whoops.

His stupidity didn't stop there. Oliver was petrified of my yellow broom. I'm specifying the color because he wasn't afraid of any other broom (we tested him with three colors), just my *yellow* broom. He would lock eyes on it and run into his crate and cower. He wasn't afraid of the horrifically loud, powerful vacuum cleaner, but if a dish towel were hanging a millimeter unevenly off of the handle on the oven door, he would bark endlessly, or until we realized *what* was causing him to freak out and fix it. I asked myself more than once if we not only had a dumb terror of a dog but one with Obsessive-Compulsive Disorder. More than once I wondered if dogs could even have OCD while I folded all of my towels the same way and stacked them by color in the linen closet. He was a strange, strange puppy.

He alternated between thinking a chair was a monster out to eat him to tearing his crate padding apart with a ferociousness comparable with the Hulk's strength. And then, he would sit and stare at me with this weird dog-grin. It was almost as if he was smiling at me while sitting in the pile of shredded crate padding as if to say, "I have no clue what the fuck happened here, but I need to take a nap so could you pop out and buy me some new crate padding? Thanks." He randomly refused to go outside to the bathroom and would flatten himself on the floor as if he wanted to win a "Laziest Bulldog In The World" award, yet he ran around the house with a speed only Usain Bolt could match. Some days, he refused to eat breakfast unless I brought it outside and placed it in the middle of a bush in the backyard. This weirdo would then back himself into the center of the bush and eat his food semi-privately, al fresco. He developed this impressive level of stubbornness where if we were trying to persuade him to do anything he didn't want to do, such as pee outside when it was early in the morning and bitter cold, Oliver would go limp. He would become dead weight, lying flat on the floor. Going limp was Oliver's strategy. And as frustrating as it was, it was also interesting because he was showing us he didn't want to make things easier for us by simply doing what we wanted him to do, yet he wasn't resisting us, either, since we could just pick him up and put him outside. Oliver was a mixture of smart and dumb, cute but ornery, and chickenshit all rolled up into one bundle of puppy. This wasn't normal, was it? How did this happen? How did we get such a defective puppy?

While some people might say this is just the way a puppy behaves, I disagree. Winnie never acted this way as a puppy. And I know, I know—all kids (and dogs) are different. Some are smart, and some are Oliver. I get it; we need differences to make the world run.

Heck, if all kids were the same there wouldn't be a use for those stupid bumper stickers that let the world know your child is smart and made the honor roll at school. Let's face it, if Oliver were a human, I most definitely wouldn't be sporting one of those stickers on my bumper. But Oliver's behavior was beyond what could be labeled as the "puppy" phase. His craziness was the "I've-come-to-steal-your-soul-by-driving-you-crazy-and-I-won't-stop-until-I've-achieved-world-domination" phase. I checked under his fur daily for a "666," and even though I couldn't find that particular demonic symbol, I felt sure we somehow ended up with a lemon of a dog. What was wrong with this thing? What happened to puppy cuddles, kisses and lovey-dovey-ness? Seriously, what the *fuck*?

What Oliver Taught Me: Life is about transition and transition doesn't happen always happen smoothly. To grow and progress in life, we need to experience what our realities are. Oliver and I were both entering new phases in our lives at the same time. While he embraced his new situations by throwing himself one hundred percent into eating my face off and seeing where it would take him, I cried and dragged my feet because I feared all of the changes I was facing, whether it was losing friends or getting a grip on my Crohn's. Maybe Oliver had the right strategy by going limp when confronted with anything he wasn't ready to face. Maybe I needed to start going limp and allow my transitions to develop into experiences and lessons instead of fearing and resisting them.

chapter
THREE

One day things changed. Oliver became calmer, quieter, less bitey and less demonic. I'm just kidding! Things became worse, and the Psycho Puppy became even more psychotic than he was before. As a day turned into weeks and weeks turned into months, the only reprieve I had from our four-legged terror was when I went to the hospital for my infusions. The nurses—who had become like sisters to me over the previous three years of treatment—loved hearing about Oliver. They thought all of his horrific terrorism was "cute" and "funny." They didn't understand I slept with one eye open just in case Oliver could catapult his fat ass onto the kitchen counter and grab a few knives with which to kill us.

One of my favorite fellow patients at the hospital, Patsy, especially loved hearing about Oliver. I met Patsy on October 14, 2007, during my first infusion. As my IV started, I began to have an anaphylactic reaction. My throat was closing, and my tongue began to swell. I was petrified because I was unable to speak. Patsy, who was an elderly gentleman with a sweet demeanor, was sitting next to me and started yelling for the nurses. They came over, stopped my infusion and got everything under control after calling my doctor and flushing my body with saline. Apparently, I was allergic to my Remicade, my infusion drug. Once I was pre-medicated with other drugs to combat my allergy to the medication, my treatment went on as planned. Patsy could see how nervous I was after that incident, so he spent the rest of our infusion time chatting with me to help distract me. Patsy and I became friends quickly from then on.

I thoroughly loved hearing his stories. And he loved hearing mine, especially those about Oliver. Patsy was eighty-two years old at that time, and it had been a long time since he owned a dog. Patsy's greetings when he saw me at the hospital were always the same: "There she is!" Despite his age and how sick he was, Patsy always had a smile on his face, his wallet tucked into his sock and a story to share. I loved every second of our hospital time together. When you have to go to the hospital for treatment as frequently as we did, you get to know the people around you—both the patients and the nurses. Patsy and I watched many people come and go from treatment, whether they had become healthy and no longer needed to be there, or because treatment failed and they were no longer with us. The only constant was that Patsy and I were always there sitting next to each other, understanding each other's pain. As time wore on and our friendship grew, we learned more and more about each other and our lives. Hell, Patsy was sitting next to me when Jimmy called to tell me Winnie had cancer. As I sat hooked up to my IV, he comforted me while I cried. We shared a bond that was rooted much deeper than just two sick people sitting next to each other in a hospital.

I'm not sure many people understood our friendship given the forty years between us, but we truly had lots in common. I looked forward to my infusions so that I could chat with him and we would often meet extra early before the infusion center was even open so that we could catch up. It wasn't long before we exchanged phone numbers and began weekly calls to check in with each other in between infusions. Patsy had several medical issues and was often in excruciating pain. That never once stopped him from being my friend or smiling while we spoke. Those talks with Patsy meant so much to me—more than I could ever describe. We discussed our health issues, our families, our homes, and our lives. We didn't expect anything from each other except for pure, unconditional friendship. When my other "healthy" friends couldn't understand what it was like living with a debilitating, incurable illness and all of the anxiety and psychological impact it was having on me, Patsy always knew because he was in a similar boat. We could easily spend an hour talking about how we missed going out to restaurants for dinner, something our illnesses prevented us from doing. Our friendship grew, and I cherished every second of it. I would offer to take him and his wife to doctor appointments or grocery shopping as it was becoming difficult for them to get around. He always turned me down. Patsy was fiercely independent and planned on being that way for a while. He didn't want anything from me—just conversation and friendship. It was important to me he knew he could call me if he needed anything. As we sat side-by-side hooked up to our IVs in a place filled with medications and sick people, we were able to both forget where we were and lose ourselves in our conversations.

We became the "Frick and Frack" of the hospital's outpatient infusion center. The nurses would try to let us sit next to each other when it was possible. He would tell me about his sons, grandkids and eventually, great-grandkids. He told me stories of his time in the Navy and proudly wore a baseball hat that had "USS Bristol DD-857," the destroyer he served on, emblazoned on it. We discussed politics, television shows, our families, spouses, health, and our doctors. We laughed a lot, and we experienced small pieces of each other's lives during our treatment times together. What a joy Patsy was in my life, especially at a time when my Crohn's prevented me from participating in most things, and I felt forgotten by many of my friends. I know most people didn't "get" the friendship we had. And that's okay; our friendship wasn't theirs to understand.

Those four-to-six hours at the hospital chatting with Patsy allowed the bleeding of all of my limbs gouged by Oliver's teeth time to heal. Patsy thought all of my Oliver anecdotes were funny, and despite the flesh wounds I suffered because of this fucked up puppy, I loved being able to make Patsy smile. Putting a smile on Patsy's face was only one benefit of my infusion times at the hospital; I relished in my time away from Hell Puppy. Then sadly, my infusion would end, and I would return to the pits of Oliver Hell, also known as "home."

Oliver never acted happy to see me come home from anywhere and never greeted us at the door the way a normal, happy puppy would. Almost every day I called Jimmy at work crying and begging to give Oliver back to the breeders. Jimmy never believed things were *that* bad, mainly because Oliver would "flip a switch," and as soon as Jimmy walked in the door from work, he was the sweetest, cutest, little muffin head. Jimmy thought I was insane. "Are you sure you aren't overreacting?" Jimmy would ask as Oliver sat on his lap, snuggling and giving him kisses filled with the love of ten million puppies. I would show him our credit card bills as proof that I had to replenish my entire wardrobe because all of my clothing had been ripped to shreds as if I'd been getting hugs from Edward Scissorhands.

As Oliver reached three months old, he adapted wonderfully to crate training, but we also wanted him to have a bed in the house. He spent nights in his crate but slept on his dog bed for naps during the day. Fears of having purchased a moose instead of a bulldog grew each time Oliver outgrew a bed, which he did twice in two weeks. Adjusting to new beds was a process because he thought we purchased beds only to satisfy his taste for destruction. It was similar to buying a kid an excellent present but having them play with the box it came in instead. He didn't get it at first.

New beds weren't the only firsts Oliver began experiencing during this time. He started walking up and down the three concrete steps into our backyard, and he began (sometimes) letting us know when he had to poop by crying at the back door. He also began to understand what the word "hungry" meant and would run to the spot where his food bowl was if I even whispered the word. Oliver also began learning some new commands, like how to "sit" when being told to sit. The fact that in two days he figured out "sit" doesn't mean bite someone's face off but rather, put your butt on the ground for three seconds and get a treat left me hopeful he was smarter than he was letting on.

Since I spent ninety-five percent of the time with Oliver while Jimmy worked, I was reaching a point where something—anything— had to be done to get this weird, fucking creep-dog to calm down, and I knew it was up to me to take the reigns and make it happen. After researching different things, we decided enrolling Oliver in "puppy school" might be a splendid idea. Our expectations were to go every Sunday for six weeks to our local chain pet store where Oliver would learn how not to be such an asshole. The bonus would be the socialization he would get with the other misfits in his class. We learned many things through having Winnie, and we were taking our first steps as dog parents to provide Oliver with the tools he needed to be the best he could be. Winnie only interacted with one other dog—a bulldog named Rosey who was several years younger than Winnie and belonged to our dear friends and neighbors, John and Terri. Unfortunately, Winnie was beyond dealing with a younger dog, so their interactions were few and far between. We wanted to make sure Oliver could interact with other dogs, especially Rosey since we were often at John and Terri's house, or they at our house. We felt some training classes with other puppies would be the best way to make that happen. To say we had high hopes that training classes would help Oliver become a nice, sweet dog would be an understatement.

We went to our first class, and there were only two other puppies enrolled—Finn and Gucci. Finn was a very shy Westie, and Gucci was a hyperactive Pitbull. Oliver fell somewhere in the middle of the two, personality-wise. The look on Oliver's face as the instructor tried to show us how to give commands and walk our dogs on a "loose leash" clearly showed he didn't know where the hell he was or what we expected him to do. So, Oliver did what he thought was appropriate: he peed all over the floor. And he didn't do it once; he did it six times. It was if he prepared for puppy school by drinking seventy-three gallons of water. I would say I was horribly embarrassed, but I think Finn's parents, Bruce and Corrine, were more embarrassed because Finn began treating Oliver's penis as his personal drinking fountain. And, unfortunately, Oliver was okay with that. In fact, he seemed to enjoy it.

As Sunday training classes came and went, Oliver learned a few things, and so did we. He learned basic commands and also earned a new nickname: the Fun Killer. Every time Gucci and Finn would play during "free time" at the end of class, Oliver would throw himself in between them and block them from playing. No dog, ever, was allowed to have fun as far as Oliver was concerned. He didn't understand "playing" at all. Puppy school ended after six weeks, and Oliver did "graduate." I use that term loosely because all he had to do was "sit" and "high five" the instructor. Not only did he do those successfully, but he also stuck his tongue out at her as he posed with his diploma. For reals. If we didn't have photographic evidence of it, I wouldn't believe it. It was Oliver's way of throwing his graduation cap in the air and saying, "Sure, I learned to sit and give you my paw, but fuck you, I'm out of here! Where's the nearest kegger?"

With puppy school under our belt, we moved on to two other pressing issues: waiting for one of Oliver's testicles to drop and teaching Oliver to stop stepping in his shit. Every day, I stared at his little puppy ball sack only to be extremely disappointed seeing one little nugget of testicle. I wanted his neutering to happen as soon as possible since humping was fast becoming his favorite thing to do. So, with Jedi mind control, I stared and stared at his ball sack until one day, I willed that fucker to drop. Oliver was finally able to be neutered, and he sailed through it with flying colors—mostly.

The actual surgery itself was flawless, and Oliver came home later that day. He was very dramatic when he realized he had to wait a few hours before eating. So, Oliver sat in front of his food bowl and howled like a wolf the entire three hours until he could get some food in his belly. Even that night, he slept well and had no pain. A few days after Oliver's neutering, he began having random bouts of vomiting. We never knew when it would happen, but it started to happen too often to ignore and continued sporadically. A trip to Dr. Denyer was in order, and after an examination and some discussion, we believed Oliver's little throat might have been a tad irritated from the tube placed in during his neutering. The chance of it clearing up on its own would probably happen, and we were to monitor him.

As Oliver turned seven months old and he healed from neutering, he was still behaving poorly. He was slightly less insane thanks to what he learned in puppy school, but still, I decided to try a new tactic. Since Oliver was now up-to-date on all of his vaccinations and healed from neutering, I decided to take the lunatic to our local park and tire the shit out of him. I would make him run and play for as long as possible. He would be too tired to eat my face off! Right? Our first few trips to the park were uneventful except for Oliver running up to garbage cans, thinking they were people. He wiggled his entire body all the way up to a trash can. The sheer look of disappointment on his face because the garbage can wasn't going to give him attention was so pathetic. He either had dreadful eyesight or an immense love for garbage. Either way, it was getting the fat bastard out of the house and distracted enough to stop chomping on my limbs like an alligator.

Early one Saturday morning we arrived at the park, and I was shocked to find a group of people with a large group of dogs. All of the dogs were off of their leashes, playing and running around. Oliver looked so small compared to all of these adult dogs; I wasn't sure what to do. One man approached me, introduced himself as Paul, and immediately told me to let Oliver off the leash, and the "pack" would show him how to behave. I took a giant leap of faith in Paul and released Oliver's leash but stayed within grabbing distance. I mentally mapped out a plan of kicking and punching this pack of dogs away from Oliver while I lifted him out of the mix and carted him back to our car should anything go wrong. Thankfully, none of that was necessary. As the dogs surrounded Oliver, they sniffed him from head-to-toe as he stood frozen to his spot. It was the only time Oliver ever looked as though he wasn't in charge. It was INCREDIBLE. I wanted to jump up and down and point in Oliver's face screaming, "BOOYAH, BITCH! HOW DOES IT FEEL TO BE NOT IN CONTROL?" Since I was in the middle of the park with a bunch of strangers, I refrained.

Auggie, the official "leader" of the pack, gave Oliver a huge once over while the rest of the dogs just huddled around. As soon as Auggie gave the "okay" by calmly walking away, Oliver was a member of the pack. Sadly, he did the same thing as he did in puppy school— he became the Fun Killer of the park. I'm certain all of these dogs instantly regretted allowing him into their group. As Callie, a beautiful Golden Retriever played with Anton, a goofy and totally lovable Weimaraner, Oliver ran at top speed and crashed into them and "broke it up." All of the dogs looked confused, and I can imagine them talking to each other in their dog language saying, "WTF is wrong with this weird-looking thing?" As seemed to be the theme with him, Oliver caused me some minor embarrassment, but I was willing to deal with it if it meant that he was going to be so tired when we went home that he would no longer desire a taste of my flesh. And it worked! We went home, and Oliver slept for roughly five hours! I had to wake him up to eat. It was the best five blood-less, clothing-in-tact hours, ever.

We returned to the park every single morning, and Oliver befriended so many dogs of all different shapes and sizes. He continued being the Fun Killer, but the dogs gave up trying to figure him out and accepted him for who he was. Oliver was the youngest member of the pack, but the sizes of the other dogs never intimidated Oliver. I would cringe with fear as Oliver would run as fast as he could before smashing head-first into the chest, flank, or ass of Jack, a very, very, large Doberman Pinscher. Oliver would bounce right off of the exceptionally well-trained Jack and then, satisfied he disrupted any fun Jack was having, would move on to his next victim. Oliver continued to be a weird puppy, ramming himself without fear into dogs four times his size, yet being completely petrified when we switched him to a raised food and water bowl. Socializing Oliver helped tame his wildebeest soul quite a bit, and it was interesting to see how the dog friends he made each played a different role in his life.

There was Callie, who allowed Oliver to be the puppy he was and climb all over her back while she patiently lied in the grass, waiting for him to finish. She was motherly towards him, often giving him her ball to chew. Anton treated Oliver the way an older brother might treat a younger brother—he would tease him relentlessly. Anton would roll Oliver over on his side and then with a ball in his mouth, rub it all over Oliver's belly as if he was tickling him or giving him a super awkward massage. Hunter, a friendly Yellow Lab, became one of Oliver's good buddies and when Oliver was in a "rough and tumble" mood, Hunter was so valuable to aid in getting Oliver to expend his energy. They played hard and rough. I always knew after some play time with Hunter, Oliver would sleep for hours. And, Oliver sleeping is a good thing because it could allow my skin heal from his shark-like bites. Other dogs taught Oliver it was wrong to steal balls and toys by giving a quick, sharp growl. Oliver was learning more from his dog friends than I could ever teach him. This rag-tag group of canine BFFs had instant bonds with each other. They ruled the park, and it was awesome to watch my weird, flesh-eating demon turn into an actual dog.

What Oliver Taught Me: Friends come in all shapes and sizes. And ages. How boring would life be if the only friends we allowed into our lives were just like us? The world would be a much lovelier place if we opened our hearts and listened to the stories people have to share with us. Embracing our differences and letting people (and dogs) into our lives is a gift. We are missing opportunities to grow and learn when we bypass or judge people who look, sound, or think differently from us.

As I watched Oliver play with all different breeds and sizes of dogs, I realized that I would never care if anyone couldn't understand my friendship with Patsy. Someone once asked me if it was depressing being friends with a "sickly old guy." Instead of replying with a quick "No," I wish I had said, "It's more depressing being friends with narrow-minded, healthy people who are my age—like you."

chapter
FOUR

While Winnie was my ride-or-die bitch from the moment of my Crohn's diagnosis in 2006 until the day we lost her, Oliver was oblivious to anything going on with me. I missed how Winnie could just sense when I wasn't feeling well. Oliver would stare at me as I ran at top speed into the bathroom so I wouldn't poop my pants. He didn't care if I was sick as long as I was still able to feed him, give him water, carry him on walks and tend to his every need. We didn't have that same weird connection that Winnie and I had. *Yet.* As time went on, my relationship with Oliver eventually morphed into a closeness that was indescribable.

Time was moving, and Oliver was growing quickly, judging by how many beds he outgrew. He still used his crate at night, but we noticed it was a little cramped as he packed on the pounds. We bought him an enormous bed—the width of a queen sized bed—and he would lie on that for naps during the day. We honestly felt crate training Oliver was beneficial, but I also didn't want a huge metal cage taking up more space in our small house. At the speed in which he was growing, Oliver would need a huge crate in which to lie comfortably. One night, we decided to see if he would sleep the entire night on his new bed located in our bedroom instead of his crate. After his final pee before bed, Oliver usually would casually walk into his crate and settle in for the night. On this particular evening, we made sure to talk loudly and try to direct his attention to our bedroom. It worked. He came running into our room, hopped onto his enormous bed and slept the entire night there. He even slept beyond his usual 5:45 am wake-up time until I woke him up at 7 am!

Another first for Oliver was a trip to the groomer's for a bath and to have his anal glands expressed, something which I would never attempt to do at home. We had used the same groomer—the Salty Dog—for all twelve years of Winnie's life and loved them so much that we knew Oliver would do well there. Instead, Oliver's first trip ended with him drawing blood from the groomer as she tried to dry him. Apparently, he didn't like the noise the dryer made and decided that sinking his razor sharp teeth into Kim's flesh would be an awesome way to let her know that. She got the message. While his behavior mortified me, Kim and everyone else at the Salty Dog understood how unpredictable puppies could be, especially when being put into unfamiliar situations. And having his anal glands cleaned for the first time was the epitome of a new situation for Oliver. This bite was gnarly and different from Oliver's typical "I-am-a-puppy-therefore-I-am-going-to-destroy-anything-that-comes-into-my-line-of-sight" bites. Kim was very understanding, and when I apologized for the nine-millionth time and vowed she would never have to lay eyes on him again, she told me I was silly, she completely understood, and would simply let Oliver air dry for the rest of his life.

Aside from drawing blood, both Kim and Barbara, the receptionist, raved that Oliver was a good boy. For a brief moment, I let myself get carried away and felt proud of my boy! This was the praise for which I had been waiting! A well-behaved dog! A dog that left people smiling! Over the years, Kim and Oliver developed a mutual understanding. She bathed him, and he allowed her to, as long as he could spend some time sitting underneath the front counter next to Barbara. Barb became Oliver's human security blanket, and while he was never a fan of going for a bath, he would still be cautiously excited to see Barb. He loved hanging out with her by the front desk instead of in the back room with the other dogs, and we would often have to beg him to leave.

After that first trip to the groomer and what we referred to from then on as "The Bite That Drew Blood," I wanted to forget all about it. I decided to reward Oliver for only biting one person instead of everyone at the Salty Dog with a trip to Petco for some new treats. He loved going to Petco so much, mostly because of the enormous amount of attention he received. Oliver believed Petco, the groomer's, the vet, and anywhere else we took him existed solely for him—the people in those places only standing by waiting for Oliver to arrive. I feel he believed the public was gathered in places, waiting to shower him with butt scratches, love, and attention. This trip to Petco wasn't any different. People crowded the store, and customers and employees alike stopped what they were doing to pet Oliver. He relished in the attention, and I was proud of how well-behaved he was being, considering only an hour earlier he had practically gnawed off Kim's hand.

Oliver decided my basking in glory was not to be tolerated and brought me down to Earth by promptly releasing any anal fluid that his anal glands had left. Have you ever smelled a dog fart before? Well, anal fluid is much, much worse. The only accurate way to describe it is if you took a five-day-old fish and covered it in shit and let it sit in the sun for twenty days. It smells fishy and foul. Walking around Petco in a funky cloud of anal fluid smell with brown funk dripping off of your dog's ass is embarrassing. It is on the same embarrassment level as being a thirteen-year-old girl who gets her period for the first time while in school on the day she decided to wear her brand new white corduroy pants. I should know. I was that girl. Both occasions had me wishing I could spontaneously combust. It was the first of many times I realized Oliver and I were alike in some odd ways. It wasn't, however, the first or last time I suffered Oliver embarrassment but it was certainly brutal. As people passed us in the store and got a whiff of him, I could feel my face reddening. I could only meet their look of displeasure by shrugging my shoulders a little and pointing down to Oliver.

As weeks went by, Oliver seemed to have turned a corner. He was no longer psychotic one hundred percent of the time. We shaved that down to about forty percent. He was finally becoming a bit more lovey-dovey. And by "lovey-dovey" I mean he stopped trying to bite off my face which was quite a relief. He became a mellower puppy and as much as I had hoped for his psychopathic ways to end, this weird calmness fucked with my head. Like, was he planning some crazy sneak attack? I was highly suspicious of this newfound niceness. Nothing much excited him. He (sometimes) seemed (mildly) happy to go to the park and play with his friends. Well, he was happy once he got there. It seemed as though all of the work of putting on his harness, getting sprayed with all natural bug spray, walking to the car, climbing into the car, enduring the one-minute car ride to the park, and then being lifted out of the car when we arrived there annoyed him. Funny, because *I* was the one doing all of the actual work and therefore, the only one who should have been irritated. Oliver was being pampered like a fucking prince, and all that was missing was a jester to make him laugh and a few burly guys waving palm fronds to keep him cool.

This new level of indifference was scary when all we had known for the first eight months was the exact opposite of it. I spent more time questioning why there was such a change than enjoying all of my limbs being mostly intact. Was it because we lopped Oliver's balls off? Was something wrong with Oliver mentally? Was he plotting world domination? Oliver became so incredibly cute and cuddly that I was alarmed. He was like the stranger with candy who drives a windowless van. He appears friendly. He has candy. He seems to want to hang out with you in his windowless van. But you know, down deep in your gut, something is *amiss*. That's what it was like living with this calmer version of Oliver.

We went from his "I-want-to-eat-your-face-off-and-I-don't-give-a-shit-I-will-even-do-it-in-public-so-don't-temp-me" phase to such mellowness so quickly; it was hard not to expect Oliver to turn back into a he-devil. He started allowing me to hug and kiss him with only minimal exorcism-worthy growling and hair eating. I remember after a particularly newsworthy cuddle session thinking, "What a fine, young gentleman-dog he is turning out to be!" I was so excited at the possibility of finally having a normal, sweet, funny, cute, and cuddly puppy. But then he would fall asleep with both eyes open, tongue out, lips pulled back into a snarl that was just mean enough to show his razor-sharp teeth, and I knew this was probably a short-lived reprieve. A girl can dream, though.

In fact, Oliver's personality change was so quick and drastic; I worried maybe he was ill. How does a flesh-eating puppy become so loving seemingly overnight? A trip to the vet for a weigh-in answered a lot of my questions. Oliver had officially changed from an English bulldog to a hippopotamus. Now weighing a whopping forty-seven pounds, this fat fucker wasn't mellowing out and becoming sweet; he was becoming a big blob who didn't have the energy to bite my face off anymore. Being evil was simply too much work for Oliver because he was plus sized.

We knew from previous experience with Winnie and all of our research on bulldogs that having an overweight bulldog is never a good thing. There is a common misperception that bulldogs should be chubby, roly-polies because all you see on television are fat, cuddly bulldogs in commercials. Think of it like this: bulldogs have all of the same stuff internally as any other "regular" sized breed, yet it is all compacted into a much smaller, oddly shaped package. Bulldogs have so many pre-disposed issues as it is; being overweight can only exacerbate those problems. We wanted Oliver to be healthy and our wonderful veterinarian, Dr. Denyer, felt that if we could keep him active, it should balance out as he grew taller and older.

So we continued our trips to the park every morning with the hopes he would run around a little and lose some weight. Oliver acted as if he was walking to the death chamber when I forced him to go each morning, yet he was still ornery enough that he refused to leave the park once we were there. He knew how it would stress me out and he enjoyed it. There were only two ways to get Oliver into the car to go home: pick him up and carry him to the car, or make EVERYBODY else leave with us. He would gladly walk to the parking lot as long as no one else was staying behind in the park. This weirdo had a severe case of "fear of missing out," or FOMO. I believe in his pea-brain, Oliver believed if I made him leave the park, there *had* to be some weird dog party the minute he left, and all of his dog friends were probably talking about him behind his back. And since carrying almost fifty pounds of dead weight across an entire park wasn't exactly fun, I would make everyone leave with us. I can't even begin to count how many times all of our friends and their dogs had to cut their park time short just because I wanted to go home. Callie's owner (Ray) would exclaim, "That's it, guys! Sherri is shutting down the park!" And we would all walk to our cars together with Oliver bringing up the rear. I felt like I was dragging a ninety-nine-year-old man around behind me.

Since Oliver seemed to be bored of the park and his friends, I thought maybe he needed a change of scenery. I decided I would start taking Oliver for walks instead of going to the park just to see if he could maybe, possibly not act like I was the worst Mom ever by trying to keep him active. Living on a busy street, the noise from the passing cars freaked him out at first, but he didn't seem bothered by it too much. We went on our first successful walk, and I was so excited! He listened, he walked beside me instead of in front of me, and he seemed to get the concept of moving just for the pure enjoyment of it. Maybe my visions of my healthy bulldog jogging five miles a day with me would come to fruition! Surely, in no time, we'd be doing marathons!

It was evident by our second walk that was never going to happen. Oliver had already grown bored. We made it only four houses away to our friends—the Bernaski's— house before he decided to stop walking. He flattened himself to the sidewalk, made himself dead weight, went limp, and refused to get up while cars honked and people yelled things out of their windows like, "I guess he doesn't want to walk today, huh?"

I was fast learning that Oliver was smart only when he wanted to be. Having been there many times by now, he knew we were in front of Terri and John's house, and he refused to move because he wanted to see them. Not only was Oliver completely in love with Terri and John and their bulldog, Rosey, but Oliver was particularly enamored with their son, Johnny. Johnny was in his early twenties, and Oliver was infatuated with him. He loved him like he loved no one else. When Oliver would see Johnny, his mind would explode with pure joy. I kind of think Johnny felt the same way about Oliver. They had a bromance that was so special. So, Oliver was not going to stand up and move because he wanted to—no, *needed* to—see Johnny. Unfortunately, Oliver didn't understand what "no one is home" meant. He had gone limp and was entirely comfortable just lying on their sidewalk, waiting for someone to come home. And so that is what we did. We waited. Once they came home, the entire Bernaski family had to escort us back to our house since it was the only way he would move. It was the first of very many Bernaski-Gibbons family parades, where I would walk Oliver to their house, visit a bit, and their entire family would walk us home.

I found myself more frustrated, depressed and annoyed about everything, whether it was Oliver-related or not, but mostly it *was* Oliver-related. I felt as if everything I tried to do with or for Oliver backfired because he was so stubborn. The dreams of having this perfect bulldog companion were disappearing before my eyes. I began to beat myself up daily. What was I doing wrong? Why wasn't any of this going the way I planned? Winnie was such an "easy" dog. Is Oliver defective? Is there a Lemon Law for bulldogs?

Clearly, walks weren't going well, and I couldn't spend six hours standing in front of the Bernaski's house without coming off as a stalker, so we went back to daily park trips since it was the lesser of two activity evils for Oliver. And just because I wanted Oliver to run and play and stay active and not weigh seven hundred pounds, he decided this would be a perfect time to become a loner. He would happily greet every person and dog friend at the park as soon as we arrived there. Then he would take someone else's ball (his ball was never good enough) and walk off by himself, put his chest on the ground, his ass in the air, roll his eyes back in his head and systematically obliterate the ball he was chewing. (We spent hundreds of dollars replacing our dog friends' balls and toys over the course of all of our park time.) This new antisocial Oliver was just as confusing as the cuddly one.

Since Winnie lived a rather sheltered life and never went to the park or socialized much with other dogs, I wasn't sure if Oliver's new loner mentality was a common thing for puppies to do as they aged. Was Oliver bored with going to the park and seeing his friends? Was he mentally unstimulated by doing the same thing every day? Or was something deeper wrong with him behaviorally? I have a tendency to beat myself up over everything, especially things and situations I know are out of my control. It is a weird, inexplicable need to be in control and when not in control, I berate myself for any outcome that isn't on par with how it would be had I been in control. So, naturally, I felt I must have been responsible for Oliver becoming the weirdo who wanted to be left alone while surrounded by tons of dog friends at the park.

I began researching as much as I could regarding the behavioral changes of a puppy and surprisingly, I couldn't find much. Of course, this had to mean I was doing something wrong! Was the food I was feeding him lacking in nutrients, causing his brain to go haywire and causing him to need to be alone? Was Oliver going to be the equivalent of the weird kid that picks his nose and eats it and never gets invited to parties? It was none of those things. Oliver only wanted to have some alone time, but he wanted it to be in the midst of a social setting to do it. After a few months of this, I was okay with it. It was his "schtick." He had a routine: he would greet every person, every dog, every garbage can, and then simply walk off and do his own thing. The expression on his face showed he loved all of the dogs and people he saw every day; he simply didn't need to be in proximity to them all of the time. And while I grew used to this new loner mentality, it meant that Oliver became less active and he started gaining more weight, which was the exact opposite of the reason we were going to the park in the first place. While I hoped this was a temporary phase and that Oliver would become more active again, he was quite content with his fast-becoming plus sized body and strutted his beefiness for everyone to see.

Since I couldn't say the same about *my* body image and because I decided I needed some personal space and time away from Oliver, I decided to join a local gym. My weight had always been an issue for me, and now having to take steroids due to Crohn's disease, I was finding it impossible to lose weight. Oliver might have been happy with his rapidly expanding waistline, but I wasn't with mine. And clearly, taking Oliver for long, fun, fast-paced walks for miles and miles around our neighborhood, making us the epitome of health like I envisioned in my head was out of the question, so I joined the gym. This was a win-win situation. I could get some time away from my defective puppy, I could lose weight, and I could even mentally feel better as I dealt with the psychological impact of having Crohn's. My Crohn's was severe enough that I need to plan everything I do down to the minute. If I was heading to the gym, that meant I couldn't have anything to eat or drink beforehand, or I would most likely crap my pants. I don't know about you, but shitting my pants in public while trying not to die on an elliptical isn't high up on my bucket list. So, I wouldn't eat, I would hit the gym and leave feeling like I was accomplishing something.

After some urging from a friend, I decided to veer further outside of my comfort zone, and I tried a spin class. I put aside my feelings of intimidation and worry that all of these super fit soccer moms would laugh when they saw the equivalent of a hippo pedaling on a spin bike and I took that first class. I was hooked! I loved being in the cool darkness of the spin room, feet flying, music pumping. Many people are surrounding you on their spin bikes, but you are also alone in the sense that you are in total darkness. It was my human version of Oliver distancing himself from the dogs at the park. I knew there were forty other people close by, yet I was alone on my bike, pedaling away, doing my own thing—just like Oliver did at the park.

After a few classes, my intimidation faded away, and I fell in love with spin classes. It helped the lights were always off so no one could see just how ridiculous I looked as I attempted my version of the bike positions. It was an excellent place for me to clear my mind and LET GO. I began taking spin classes five-to-six days a week. Several spin instructors warned me that I was overdoing it, but it felt too good to stop. So, I kept going and pushing myself, burning over seven hundred calories an hour and losing some weight—something that doesn't come easy when you are on steroids. That frenzied pace lasted for a couple of weeks and then I began feeling pain in my right knee.

At the same time, after a play session at the park, Oliver began randomly limping on his right hind leg. He would do it after running and then five minutes later, be perfectly fine. After a couple of days of this, I limped my way on *my* gimpy knee to let Dr. Denyer take a look at *Oliver's* gimpy knee. She examined him and told us that Oliver had a kneecap that liked to pop out. It was very easy to push back into place gently, and Dr. Denyer also explained that very often, it would fall back into place on its own and gave us some exercises such as having him lie down while we stretched out his leg. We would monitor it as time went on. We laughed and made a few jokes that Oliver was mirroring me since we were both dealing with issues with the same knee. It wasn't the first sign of a weird connection we had with each other, but it was the first medical parallel we shared.

As we carefully monitored Oliver's gimpy kneecap, a new issue began. Oliver started vomiting every time we stepped into the park. It started one day out-of-the-blue, and the first time it happened, I didn't think much of it. Then it happened the second day. Without fail, as soon as we stepped out of the car and into the park, it was as though some demonic presence entered his body. Vomit spewed out of his mouth and caused all of his dog friends and their owners to scatter. The strangest thing is that he would puke horribly once or twice, and then he was fine for the remainder of our park visit. And, he was always fine all day at home.

On the third day, once again, Oliver decided to christen the park in puke. I called Dr. Denyer as soon as we returned home and made an appointment so we could troubleshoot the issue. As I explained our latest problem to Dr. Denyer, I learned what Oliver was doing wasn't technically considered vomiting. It was regurgitation. Most of his kibble was being spat out undigested. So, we tried to be logical. Oliver drinks water while at the park. If he has eaten breakfast before going, could the water cause the kibble to expand since he virtually inhaled his food rather than chewed it, thereby causing him to regurgitate? Oliver's exam went great, and despite packing on more pounds, Dr. Denyer couldn't quite figure out what would cause him to regurgitate while at the park. She suggested trying different feeding routines to see if they would help.

First, I tried holding off his breakfast until after the park. On that day, he spewed bile that was of *Exorcism* proportion. I apologized profusely while picking up vomit and bile with a doggy poop bag and kicking dirt over whatever was too liquefied to get up. There was always that one weird dog, usually Hunter, who liked to eat Oliver's vomit which would freak out everyone. He would munch on it while myself and his owner, Donna, would scream at him to stop. He would then run over and lick whatever spit strings of vomit-drool were left hanging from Oliver's jowls. As gross as it was, I took comfort in knowing I didn't have the only weird dog at the park. Since delaying his breakfast didn't help that day and bile came up, it was obvious he needed to eat before playing. We tried giving him water in smaller increments while playing at the park and that didn't help. We tried breaking his breakfast into two portions, one before the park and one after. That seemed to help a little but not enough for me to not be embarrassed as everyone ran away from us as undigested kibble spilled out of Oliver's face. As with many issues that had yet to develop, Oliver's vomiting, just like his gimpy back leg, was something we would have to monitor.

What Oliver Taught Me: You need to be okay with yourself. You need to be okay with saying, "I need some ME time." Somewhere throughout time, we have lost the ability to be okay with being alone and doing things for ourselves. We attach guilt to these acts. People will say, "I'm going to spoil myself!" or "I am going to treat myself!" Since when did doing something by ourselves, or for ourselves, become something we needed to justify? We deserve alone time and we shouldn't ever feel bad about it.

So, do whatever it takes—whether it is huffing and puffing your way through a scary spin class, or sitting alone in a park chewing a ball (Gosh, I'd be worried about you if that's what you did!). Be okay with being alone and doing something that allows you to shut down from the stresses and chaos life can sometimes bring. Really. It's *okay* to tune out a little. It's good for your soul.

chapter
FIVE

Each time a medical situation would arise with Oliver, such as his regurgitation and knee problems, I would contact the breeders to see if they could provide any evidence of a genetic issue, or even offer some advice or input. With both of Oliver's main medical issues—the regurgitation and the floating kneecap—we were told Oliver's parents experienced neither issue. While Patti and Michael weren't able to help with his medical issues, they were instrumental in bringing us together with Oliver's sister. We found out through the breeders that a family who lived only one town over from us had his sister, Henrietta! Patti and Michael gave us their contact information, and I instantly emailed the puppy's owner, Laura Alvarez. As we exchanged emails, we laughed at the fact that our cute little puppies had names that made them sound like senior citizens. Oliver and Henrietta needed to meet up. We emailed many times getting to know each other and planned our first meet up at Laura's house a few months before their first birthday.

We were so excited to meet Henrietta and her family! We hadn't seen her since the first time we laid eyes on all three puppies in the litter at the Rathje's house. What a crazy, funny time we had the Alvarez's home. Henrietta was much, much smaller than Oliver. He outweighed her by twenty pounds, yet Henrietta was clearly in charge. She instantly pinned him to the living room floor while he pretended to bite her face. They were crazy, out of breath, and we all agreed they clearly remembered each other. There isn't any doubt in my mind; they shared an instant intimate bond. I saw it; Jimmy saw it and Laura saw it, too. There wasn't any hesitation the way there usually is when two dogs meet for the first time. Henrietta and Oliver played and ran and enjoyed each other's company, just as we enjoyed Laura's company and meeting her family. What a wonderful blessing to know that Oliver and his sister could get together from time-to-time, as well as allow us to make some new, sweet friends who fell in love with Oliver as we had with Henrietta.

What struck me as fascinating was Laura told me that when she was younger, she always knew she would have a white English bulldog and name her Henrietta. I believe in the Power of Intention and Law of Attraction, and I felt Henrietta showing up in Laura's life was a perfect example of both. And, while we might flippantly say something which we truly mean in our hearts, it is heard and put out into the universe. I believe Henrietta chose the Alvarez family just as much as I think Oliver chose us. The fact that Laura knew she would one day have a white bulldog only reinforced my belief in there not being coincidences in life, only synchronicity. And Jimmy and I were meant to meet Laura and her family through these beautiful bully siblings and be in each other's lives for a reason. We might not have known what that reason was at the time, but there is always a reason things play out they way they do.

The Alvarez family was such a lovely family and Henrietta fit right in with her new human parents and siblings. I began referring to her as the "little peanut" because she was so delicate and dainty compared to the five hundred pound walrus that was Oliver. Henrietta and Oliver were different genders and different colors and different weights, yet their faces were identical. It was so wonderful to see Oliver drop his loner status when in Henrietta's presence. It didn't surprise me that Henrietta dominated Oliver; in the very first pictures I received of them at three weeks old, Henrietta had her head strategically placed on top of Oliver in every picture. They knew their roles. Henrietta was in charge.

Fall approached, and suddenly it was already Oliver's first birthday on November 1, 2011. I couldn't believe he was one year old already. Oliver celebrated his birthday by playing at the park with a bunch of friends, eating, napping, making a visit to Petco—all of which were fun, exciting things. Just when I was ready to exclaim Oliver's first birthday as a special day, he ruined it all by throwing up and then stepping in his poop. At least he was consistent. And, as soon as Oliver's first birthday passed, it was as though a wave of calmness came over him. It was strange, and I was very excited that he was "on schedule"—as far as Google was concerned—to becoming the fine, sweet gentleman-dog I knew he could be. He went from being forty percent satanic to about thirty percent evil. If you're keeping track, we seemed to be dropping in evilness at an alarmingly slow rate. But, this was still progress! This new level of niceness left me hopeful that by his second birthday, he would hopefully only be fifteen percent wicked. A girl can dream, right? I mean, at least he was headed in the right direction.

That brief reprieve from Oliver's rambunctious ways didn't last, however. In fact, one week after his first birthday things changed quickly and Oliver regressed behaviorally. He became jealous anytime I tried to pet another dog. I use the word "try" because it truly was an effort; Oliver refused to let me touch any other dog. Ever. He would use his massive body as a battering ram and plow into whichever dog I was trying to pet. Oliver would then position himself between me and any other dog who he deemed unworthy of my attention so my hands could only reach him. I was his human, and he wanted every dog on Earth to know it. He also tore a few magazines to shreds and began trying to hump Jimmy often. These were not behaviors we had seen from him before. It was perplexing.

The biggest and most frustrating change in Oliver at this time, however, was he began putting into practice selective listening. He refused to listen. If I called his name, he ignored me. If I asked him to sit, stay, come, or be quiet, he ignored me. Even my threats of letting all of his friends know he still peed like a girl didn't phase him. He didn't give a shit. At all. It was as though a light bulb went off above his head and he thought, "Hey. I could just not listen. What is *she* going to do about it?" This new round of obnoxious behavior had one benefit: he was so tired by 1:15 pm from not listening and misbehaving, he would crash fast, and I was able to take a short nap so I could rest up for the remainder of the day with him.

One of the best things about Oliver at this time was that even though he was an expert at selective listening, he could no longer pull off some of the rambunctious puppy hijinks he did months ago. He was bigger, clumsier, louder, and a little bit of a pussy if he knew he might get into trouble. Oliver thought he was cute and funny and sneaky, but he wasn't. For as many times as I saw Oliver try to do something he wasn't supposed to do, there had been an equal amount of occasions that he botched it up before he could reap the self-satisfaction of pulling off a successful caper. Oliver didn't like being reprimanded by me, at all. He didn't care if Jimmy raised his voice, but he couldn't tolerate if I did. Maybe it was because Oliver and I spent more time together and he didn't want to disappoint me. Or, perhaps I just sounded scarier.

For example, one night I had left my slippers on the living room floor, and one of my socks was haphazardly lying on top of one of the slippers approximately a foot-and-a-half away from where Oliver was lying. Since Oliver had outgrown his teething stage, he had stopped shredding my clothing. Still, there was something about that sock that enticed him. He *wanted* that sock. *He needed that sock.* Inch by inch, Oliver pulled his body closer using only his front legs very s-l-o-w-l-y over to the sock, without ever standing up. He did these super small movements believing I didn't see him getting closer to the sock. I did see them. I watched and waited to see what he would do, and sure enough, he picked the sock up in his mouth with the intention of eating it. I raised my voice slightly and said, "OLIVER, NO!" His nerves got the better of him, and he proceeded to throw up all over the sock and both slippers. We established a new quirk: the slightest raise in my voice would cause Oliver to puke. I never even had to be loud; even the most minor change to an authoritative tone would do the trick, and he would puke. It was incredible and awful all at the same time. Wielding such power and finally having him listening to me was fantastic! Having to clean up dog vomit, not so much.

As January 2012 hit us, so did the thick of winter. Oliver loved the snow as did most of our dog friends from the park. The snow must have had a magical power over Oliver because he abandoned his loner ways and had a lot of fun running through it, picking up clumps of it in his mouth, and having a blast while I froze my ass off and complained about standing in the middle of the park in freezing temperatures. While it was so sweet to see him being social again, I couldn't help but seethe that he chose to do so when it was so damn cold out. I felt it was my duty to keep him social and active, so if playing in near-freezing temperatures would tire him out, so be it.

Bundling up with waterproof snow boots, layers of sweatshirts, thermal pants under jeans, two or three pairs of socks, and two pairs of gloves just so my weird dog could play in the snow for ten minutes seemed a little ridiculous to me. All of the owners would huddle together and complain about how cold we were while our dogs ran around and acted as if each time they saw snow was the first. Oliver never lasted long because I was so concerned about his feet becoming too cold. I tried buying dog snow booties, and after struggling for thirty minutes, sweating under my three thousand sweatshirts trying to get them on Oliver's huge paws, he would promptly kick them off of his feet within the first four seconds of having them on. I had hoped those booties would allow him to play longer to justify us even being out in such weather. Since the booties didn't work, each morning we would trudge through the snowy field so that Oliver could run in circles for ten minutes. It was ridiculous, but it did tire him out, and we all know a tired Oliver is a calmer Oliver! We would come home from the park, and after I would peel my layers of clothing off and dry Oliver with a towel, he would snuggle on his bed, warm and safe and happy and tired. Ollieman loved his friends, the park, and the snow—but he also enjoyed coming home to his lovely warm house and bed. The look in his eyes as he curled up on one of his beds after being outside in the snow was a look of pure thankfulness and bliss.

While Oliver was enjoying winter, and I was complaining how cold it was at the park every morning, I was gently reminded of how fortunate we were even to have a home in which to live. A childhood friend had posted on Facebook that she was beginning a collection of clothing, essentials such as soap and toothpaste, and non-perishable food for a local homeless camp, known to us as Tent City. I became reacquainted with my childhood friend as adults, thanks to Facebook. She had come to know the person who was primarily in charge of Tent City, who was a pastor, and felt she needed to do more to help the people living there. Tent City was home to many people at the time. These were people from all walks of life; people who had fallen upon hardships and had come together to form a camp where they lived as a community. My friend's post on Facebook, calling for help and compassion, was the reminder I needed to be grateful and to give. I instantly contacted her and asked how I could help. We began posting on social media, asking for donations, and we were pleasantly surprised at how many people came together to help. I had designated one shelf in one of our spare rooms as a "collections" shelf as friends and family began dropping off clothing, toothbrushes, soap, canned food, and other essentials. That shelf quickly filled, and I was euphoric as donations began to take over my house. Several local businesses opened their doors to receive donations, and we were very grateful to everyone who was so earnestly willing to help.

A group of us had a caravan of cars and vans filled with donations, and when we made our first delivery, meeting the pastor and the other residents was a humbling moment. The people of Tent City welcomed us and the gratefulness for our donations was clearly shown on every face. We spent time meeting the residents, and we listened to stories about how some of them came to live there. They showed us around their camp and the kindness they showed us was something I don't think I will ever forget. These are people who were just barely scraping by, yet the pride they took in their homes was something that struck me. Some had decorated the outside of their makeshift tents; some had gardens planted so they would have vegetables to eat. All welcomed us with open arms. If only we could all be so kind! The gratitude they showed us as we unloaded our cars was something very special, and I considered myself lucky to have been a part of helping.

We went on to support Tent City with several more rounds of donations through the winter and took on the particular challenge of raising money to replace their log splitter that was, sadly, stolen. Keeping warm through the winter months wasn't a luxury for the people of Tent City; it was a necessity. They didn't have the option of walking around the snow and then simply going inside to blast their heat, drink some hot chocolate and warm up. We started spreading the word on social media about the stolen log splitter, and once again, the outpouring of help was incredible—this time in the form of financial donations. We were able to deliver over $1,400 to the Tent City community to replace the stolen log splitter. As we continued to do monthly collections and drop-offs, the township filed a lawsuit against Tent City, trying to evict them. There were concerns about safety, fire liability and other issues the town outlined in their lawsuit. It was an on-going battle between the town and the residents that, sadly, ended a couple of years later with Tent City being torn down, forcing the homeless out. My very, very, *very* small part in helping the residents of Tent City will always have a lasting impact on my life. And while some of us who came together to help Tent City have drifted apart, the opportunity to do some good for people in need will always connect us.

What Oliver Taught Me: Donating clothing, toiletries, food and money are always beautiful things to do, but I encourage you to give time, also. Seeing how people live and how they are struggling will impact you and will only enforce your drive to do more to help. Someone may be less fortunate than you but that does not mean they are less human. Having the chance to speak with and connect with the people you are helping is so rewarding.

The next time I stood in the park freezing so Oliver could play with his friends took on a new meaning. I stopped complaining. I could leave that park and return to a home that had heat and where being hungry is solved with a few short steps to the refrigerator. And after playing in the snow and watching Oliver snuggle up in his warm bed, sighing in between snores, I realized I needed to remember to be grateful, kind, and fully appreciate of all I've been given in life. It is so easy to take for granted the things we have become so used to having. It is okay to enjoy life, and it is okay to benefit from the things in your life, but do so with gratefulness because there is always someone who has much less.

chapter
SIX

As the winter of 2012 began to fade into the early stages of spring, Oliver started limping again on his right hind leg. After another trip to Dr. Denyer, she suggested we take him for an exam at a veterinary hospital a short drive north of us on the Garden State Parkway, as she suspected Oliver might have torn his Cranial Cruciate Ligament, or CCL. Since we weren't able to get an appointment before the end of April, Dr. Denyer suggested Oliver should stay home from the park, and we limit his activity until his appointment at the hospital. Having to rest and not be too active was Oliver's dream come true. He kicked his napping and laziness up a notch, and while we were happy he was okay with being lazier than usual, the lack of exercise triggered insomnia in Oliver. Yes, you read that correctly: our bulldog had insomnia.

Oliver would sleep most of the day since we were limiting his activity and then every night, around 1:00 am, he would begin walking around the house, looking for toys. Have you ever heard a dog's nails clicking on hardwood floors all night long? It is unbelievably annoying! Click, click, tap, click, tap—for hours! Oliver's insomnia, and therefore my insomnia by proxy, went on for almost a month. Trying to keep him awake, yet inactive, during the day was an impossible task. I would speak to him regularly each time it looked as though he was ready for a daytime nap and the look of complete annoyance on his face never went unnoticed on my end. The beautiful part of all of this was that it was as though someone flipped a switch and psycho puppy understood he needed to calm the fuck down. Our weird, mean, little guy settled into a softer, more loving, lazy bastard. While the insomnia phase was hard to deal with, it was worth it since I wasn't having my face bitten off all day long. We had turned a corner, and Oliver was finally growing up. His psycho puppy status had finally dropped to zero percent!

Finally, at the end of April 2012, our appointment at the veterinary hospital arrived and simply by feeling Oliver's left hind leg, the doctor determined that even though he didn't show any signs of pain or discomfort, he had torn his CCL and would require surgery. We could elect not to have surgery, but that would increase the chances of Oliver developing arthritis as he grew older. We certainly didn't want that, so we opted for surgery—and I began the panic and anxiety filled task of researching the type of surgery Oliver would be having, all it entailed, as well as what we could expect during his recovery.

Oliver was going to have Tibial Tuberosity Advancement or TTA surgery. TTA surgery works by changing the way the quadriceps pull on the tibia. It would correct that and seemed the most efficient way to repair Oliver's torn CCL. As my anxiety over this situation set in, I busied myself researching the surgery and watching it being done to dogs via videos on YouTube. I suggest you never, ever do that. I was so stressed and worried about Oliver having to undergo anesthesia along with the surgery itself; I knew if I didn't know every detail of what it would entail, I wouldn't sleep for the two weeks leading up to his surgery. So, gory videos seemed like the best choice. It wasn't.

Reading up on the recovery phase was daunting, especially since it was going to be a three-month process. Oliver was going to have to be contained either in his crate or in our bedroom, where there was wall-to-wall carpeting, versus the rest of the house that had hardwood floors and could cause him to slip and re-injure himself. Already cramped in his crate, Oliver was a total porker, so we had to buy an even bigger crate—something I had been desperately avoiding. We also began practicing towel-walking, which is when you take a large towel, position it under the dog's belly and around its middle. You then lift your pup's hind legs up using the ends of the towel, so it doesn't put weight on its hind legs. We were hoping to use this method when Oliver needed to go outside to the bathroom. Testing this means of aiding Oliver in walking went over without a hitch. Just kidding! Oliver froze as soon as we wrapped the towel around his belly and gave us a Death Stare that chilled us to our bones. I spent every minute of every day in panic mode with the stress of his impending surgery making me break out into cold sweats every fifteen minutes.

That panic and worry caused my Crohn's to flare up like an angry beast. Truthfully, my Crohn's wasn't under control anyway, but this added stress caused my body to go even more haywire. In the two weeks from finding out Oliver needed surgery until the day of the actual surgery, I had to reach out to my gastroenterologist three times for help. My frequent trips of running to the bathroom with uncontrollable diarrhea went from five to seven times per day to over ten times per day. Nothing about me has ever been "normal," and this round of stress-related Crohn's bullshit wasn't any exception. If living with as little stress as possible can significantly reduce Crohn's symptoms, then I fully expected to implode any day during those two weeks. Thankfully, I only shit my pants twice and both times were while I was at home. Small blessings.

Finally, Oliver's surgery day arrived. I was worried he wouldn't do well with the anesthesia since having regurgitation issues after having gone under anesthesia for his neutering. But, we needed to do what was best for our little curmudgeon. The hospital was going to keep him overnight which brought me a little relief as far as taking care of him immediately after surgery. I began to think ahead and boy, was I worried about how things would be when he came home from the hospital. I was one hundred percent convinced that while he would be in *some* pain, Oliver would undoubtedly become very dramatic. He would make me feel as though he had his leg cut off instead of just a small incision and that I was the person who cut it off and then hung it over the fireplace mantle as a trophy. Oliver could be very theatrical for a dog. If we even so much as sprayed a little of his doggy cologne on him, he would run and smash his body into the furniture. Because of *cologne*. I could only imagine how dramatic he would be with an incision and stitches.

Dropping Oliver off at the hospital for his TTA surgery was tough for me. I was a chaotic mix of anxiety, stress, and yet down deep, I knew it was what was best for Oliver in the long run. His surgery went well, and the hospital called just as he was waking up. My nervousness shifted from the worry of the actual surgery to nervousness about how we could keep him calm, contained, and happy once he came home the next day. I needn't have worried; Oliver was sleepy and not in much pain when we brought him home the following day. He was perfectly happy lying on his bed, taking long pain-killer induced naps and being carried like a prince to his bowls for food and water. While the Prince of Silverton enjoyed the attention, I was so stressed out about Jimmy returning to work and having to take care of my gimpy dog alone, that I proceeded to shit my pants a few more times for good measure.

Oliver took his recovery in stride. Within five days of surgery, he began "toe-touching," where he would tap his foot to the ground, testing to see if he could bear weight on his leg. Another few days later and Oliver was successfully hopping down the few stairs we had out back to go to the bathroom and hobbling around without a care in the world. I, naturally, remained in a state of panic and anxiety.

What once sounded like an insanely long recovery time of three months, breezed by quickly. Oliver received lots of attention, plenty of treats, lots of bones to keep him busy, and lots of love. He flourished, while the stress caused me to shit my pants daily. Literally. He took each day as it came and only did what he felt capable of doing. Why was I not living like Oliver in these moments?

What Oliver Taught Me: Stress is an evil emotion. It wreaks havoc on our minds and bodies and is completely unnecessary. Life is going to happen whether we freak out or not. Becoming nervous and riddled with anxiety isn't beneficial. And, I believe that fear and anxiety over certain situations tend to be more troublesome than the situations themselves. Those fears and anxieties cause us to react— whether we cry, have panic attacks, lash out at people unintentionally, or shit our pants. The build-up of anxiety waiting for an uncontrollable outcome adds a layer of negativity that our minds, bodies, and spirits do not need.

We need to trust there is a greater plan and stop wasting energy on negative emotions. There will always be "speed bumps" on the roads we travel in our lives. Successfully navigating them is much easier when we have faith, are calm—and believe in ourselves, our decisions, and the people we love.

chapter
SEVEN

October of 2012 marked significant changes for us—not for anything fun or pleasant—but because of a couple of stressful situations. First, after experiencing some gynecological issues and being sent for an ultrasound, I was told my doctor saw "something" on one of my ovaries. When a doctor uses such an undefined term medically such as the word "something," that leaves your mind wide open to imagining it is "EVERYTHING." My gynecologist wanted me to repeat the test as soon as possible. When I spoke to her on that Friday, we left it as I would swing by her office on Tuesday to pick up a prescription for a retest. Unfortunately, Mother Nature sent our lives into upheaval before I could even worry about my gimpy ovary.

For several days, all eyes were on the weather as Hurricane Sandy was getting closer to making landfall. There still wasn't enough certainty where the Sandy would land, or how much of an impact it would make. With our neighborhood surrounded on three sides by water, our local fire department began asking residents to move their vehicles to higher ground on Sunday, October 28, 2012, before Sandy was to make landfall the following evening. We went through the typical protocol that most people do when there are weather events: we watched the news with casual indifference, and we went to the grocery store to stock up on snacks. The milk and bread aisles were barren, so we were pretty grateful the cookie aisle was well stocked. We had our priorities straight. We then went to our local home improvement store because we figured if the grocery store's milk and bread aisles were even a little empty—the indicator by which humans judge the severity of all natural disasters—it might be smart to have a flashlight in case we lost power for a few hours. We weren't the only people who had that idea; the shelves were bare of just about anything that could help in a storm. From batteries to flashlights to generators, the store looked as if it had already been through a hurricane.

After Hurricane Irene a year prior was a non-event that had spurned a lot of unnecessary panicking, I wasn't sure if our local government was overreacting by telling us we had the option to evacuate and that we should move our cars to higher ground for this hurricane. I started to feel uneasy when as Sunday went on, the government instructed people who lived on the barrier island five minutes from us that they were under a strict mandatory evacuation. I talked myself out of worrying and had made myself feel okay about staying home, but then Jimmy had a change of heart. His car was new. It even still smelled new. Our driveway tends to flood a little. He felt we should move our vehicles, or at the very least, his new-smelling one. Two locations nearby were set up for the community to park their cars. As we were deciding which one to park at, my parents called because they were concerned with our safety since we lived two streets from the water. They talked us into evacuating to their house with both of our cars and Oliver on Monday morning, about twelve hours before Sandy was due to make landfall.

With one of Oliver's beds, some of his favorite toys and bones, a couple of articles of clothing and a few essentials for us, we camped out at my parents' house in a local retirement community. Despite being in the same town as us, they lived about twenty minutes away and further inland. When Hurricane Sandy made landfall, winds were high, and rain poured down, but aside from a short one-hour loss of electricity and a few tree branches falling on my parents' property, not much appeared to have happened. The following morning I received a text message from my sweet friend Turi Thatcher who lived near us, but further from the water. She texted me that things were terrible in our neighborhood. She told me she tried to drive to my house to check on it for us, but the torrential rain had flooded our street so badly that EMS, the police, and fire departments were using boats and jet skies to rescue people—by driving the vehicles on the street. Turi tried in the gentlest of ways to tell me that while she couldn't drive too closely to my house because of the streets being flooded, she could see from a distance that our house had taken on water. Because we weren't there and I couldn't physically see what she had described to me, my brain couldn't register that actual boats were driving down the streets. I couldn't wrap my mind around the water being that high—or our house having been affected.

My Dad drove us to our house in his pickup truck to check out the damage for ourselves. As we left the community my parents lived in and drove into our part of town, it was as if we had arrived in a different country—one that was submerged underwater. As we approached our home, I could not believe what I was seeing. Cars were freely floating down the roads; there wasn't any power, so street lights weren't working. We couldn't get anywhere near our home as jet skis and rescue boats traveled in many feet of water up and down the road. Jimmy and I hopped out of the truck and waded in thigh-deep water to our house. Before even opening the front door, it was clear that we had most likely lost everything as the water surge was over four feet deep, destroying the trees and fencing around our house.

Stepping inside the front door was devastating. Furniture, shoes and random household items were floating from room-to-room. There was water, sand, and sediment everywhere. While Jimmy surveyed the damage in what I can only describe as a complete shock, I lost my shit and became hysterical. We have never lived a grand life. We have always been grateful for what we have, but financially, we always had flown by the seat of our pants. To see what little we did have floating through the house, I couldn't even process the possessions we lost, much less the damage the storm had done to our house itself. I don't think I have ever felt so helpless and at a loss of what to do.

In a moment where you can't even process how much material possessions you've lost, that loss becomes secondary. Things are things. The extras in life—TVs, computers, video game systems, cameras, furniture—we could replace those. The loss of thousands of photos, of my wedding dress, the walls of our house—that loss is crushing. Completely crushing. All I could think about was how would we ever, ever, ever repair our house? How could we live here? How long would we be not able to live in our cute little house and live our normal lives? In a time like this, such an unfamiliar and fear-inducing situation, you do not know what to do first.

The water hadn't yet receded, so we knew that attempting to save anything was useless. Grabbing flood insurance and homeowner insurance papers was our only goal, and thankfully, we were able to get to them. We waded in water that was hip-deep back out to my father's truck. It wasn't even twenty-four hours after the hurricane, and news crews and people whose homes faired better than ours filled our neighborhood, coming for a look at the damage. There wasn't any electricity, so our friends and neighbors didn't even know how the rest of the town, or even the East Coast as a whole, had made out. Our tiny community of Silverton was one of the hardest hit by Hurricane Sandy. Houses along the bay were gone. Gone! Cars were floating everywhere as if they were toys, yet you could drive two minutes in any direction, and everything was fine, houses unscathed. It's difficult to feel happy for people whose lives hadn't changed while we were facing everything being completely different. We drove away feeling sick, sad, and petrified of learning just how bad the damage to our home would be once the water receded.

In the midst of figuring out how to progress in those first few hours after the hurricane hit, I realized I would also need to get to my gynecologist's office to pick up the prescription to have the re-imaging of my ovary done. In between phone calls to our insurance companies and since we couldn't do anything at our house until the water receded, I continuously tried to call my doctor's office, which was located one town over. Brick Township was also hit very hard by the hurricane. My gynecologist's office didn't have electricity, just as there wasn't any in Silverton. I was walking a fine line between sanity and insanity, worrying about my home, our future, and my fucking ovary. My ever-faithful Crohn's kicked in high gear, and I lost twelve pounds in less than two weeks. (Keep an eye out for my next book, *The Hurricane Diet*.)

I believed if I could get the test retaken, I would be okay and that would be one less stressor in my life. I took a leap of faith and decided to drive to my doctor's office to see if they were possibly there but didn't have phone lines working. A twenty-minute drive turned into a two-hour trek. Since many street lights were still not working and water still flooded most roads, there were detours everywhere, and cars lined up for miles trying to get gas at every gas station that was open. Meanwhile, I sat in traffic alternately crying and screaming at the cars all around me. I needed a break. Just one break, a small miracle that I could get to my doctor's office, pick up the prescription for my tests and I knew I would feel better. Of course, that didn't happen. After two hours and many screamed swear words, I arrived at the medical building where my doctor's office is located to find the entire parking lot turned into a triage center where ambulances and F.E.M.A. tents were set up. The whole parking lot was closed off, so I began my two-hour journey back to my parent's house.

It took almost twenty-four hours for the water to recede due to several phases of high tides. When we made our way back to our home, with the water now mostly gone, the devastation was beyond comprehension. We entered our house and began throwing whatever was salvageable into garbage bags. We needed clothing and personal items. We grabbed what we could and loaded my father's truck as many people who were eager to see the damage to our neighborhood watched. I was furious. Here we were, scraping up the few belongings we have left, and random people from other communities stood taking pictures of us. The lack of compassion only deepened the despair we felt. It's human nature to be curious. I'm not above slowing down and looking at a car crash as I drive by one. However, I wouldn't purposefully drive to the scene of a wreck just to take some photos of it. That's what it felt like to me—these people who didn't even know us, know our lives, would be sitting around the dinner table talking about watching us taking garbage bags of a few possessions we had left out of our home. Hurricane Sandy violated us; random people using our devastation to sight-see violated us even more.

Unable to even rent a U-Haul or POD storage unit since none were available, we made several trips using my Dad's pickup truck and our two cars and tried to salvage everything we could, filling my parents' garage with our belongings. We then relied on my two aunts, who allowed us to use their garages to store more things.

The feeling of loss is indescribable when you begin to pick up and touch your belongings and see them destroyed beyond saving. We were lucky to save clothing that was hanging in our closets and anything in our kitchen that had been in the upper cabinets. I began the tedious task of washing load after load of clothes that were soaking wet and covered in mud, trying to salvage what I could. It's surreal to think that things we loved and used every day were now simply garbage. When you don't have a lot of money, and you lose almost everything, it is very easy to sink so deep into despair. It was difficult for me to balance my feelings when I felt awful losing so much, yet felt guilty for feeling that way when there were so many people who lost more than us. Each day, I tried to process how I felt and would give up and just try to let things be. It isn't easy to let things be, especially for an O.C.D. control freak like me.

Since the township instructed the community to start lining up our garbage in front of our houses, it began to pile up everywhere, making it difficult for people to drive in our neighborhood. Neighbors began to complain as traffic started to build on our narrow streets with people hanging out of their cars taking photos of houses that were barely standing. It was so wrong and so hurtful. Thankfully, our local police department set up multiple locations every few streets and began checking identification. You now had to be a resident to enter our neighborhood. This rule wasn't in place solely to help us functionally or even emotionally, but also because people were breaking into damaged, empty homes at night and looting anything they could get their hands on—televisions, copper wiring, medications. It was disgusting. Some even went so far as to travel by boat to houses along the bay to avoid the police checkpoints.

There wasn't any electricity in Silverton, so they came and stole whatever they wanted under cover of darkness. Our local Toms River Police Department did a fantastic job of squelching the looting, and we felt extra lucky one of the checkpoints was directly in front of our house. As the days went on, the neighborhood rallied behind these officers who were outside our homes protecting us twenty-four hours a day by doing small things like bringing them coffee, water, and food. When you lose so, so much you are so grateful for even the smallest acts of kindness. The Silverton community supported each other and we were just as grateful for that as we were for my parents taking us into their home.

Thankfully, my Dad had been flipping houses for several years and had the knowledge of which steps we needed to take next. After getting permission from our insurance agency, we were able to begin the long and painful process of gutting our house, as long as we photographed every step of it. The fact that we waded through water immediately after Sandy hit to grab our insurance papers was the smartest thing we ever did. It allowed us a leg up on many people since we called hours after the hurricane blew by, instead of days after like many people did. We considered ourselves lucky; our house was still standing, and the structure was intact. Sure, we were going to have to tear all the way down to the sub-flooring and up four feet of the walls, but many homes surrounding us were no longer standing.

Our first order of business was to clean out the house. We knew this was going to be a big job and we began calling people for help. We were fortunate to have help from my uncle and our friend Tom, along with my Dad. We met early in the morning and began the process. While I hauled our damaged belongings to the curb with help from my Uncle Johnny and Tom, Jimmy and my Dad started peeling the layers of our house away beginning with the flooring. Carpeting—saturated with water and sand—had to be cut into small, rollable pieces due to how heavy they were and carted out to the curb by hand truck. Wood flooring underneath was already showing signs of mold growth within those few days due to the salt water. In front of our house, a wall of garbage that was almost five feet high quickly filled the curb. Garbage trucks had yet to begin making rounds, so we began to fill the front lawn with more garbage. Anything inside that was metal, such as our refrigerator, was a loss as the salt water was going to cause it to rust. Our water heater, boiler, central air conditioning unit—all lost. And all expensive to replace. Thankfully, we had flood insurance on the structure of our house, just not on our personal belongings. We constantly tried to remind ourselves as we carried our belongings out front to the garbage pile to be grateful our house was standing, and we were safe. We can replace things. And boy, was there a lot of stuff we lost. Furniture both inside and outside, a lawn mower, snow blower, grill, forks, knives, spoons, appliances, and furnace—everything was a loss.

A few days after Hurricane Sandy I was scheduled for an infusion at the hospital, which was still running on the emergency generators. I needed my treatment to keep functioning at such a stressful time, so I went on my scheduled day. Another reason I went was that I hadn't been able to contact Patsy after the hurricane and I was very concerned about him. I was hoping he would be there for his infusion, also. Patsy and his wife lived right on the bay in Lavallette, located on the barrier island. The state of New Jersey ordered a mandatory evacuation for his little beach community, and despite having two sons who both lived inland in Toms River, I suspected Patsy wouldn't have evacuated. I was right.

When I arrived at the hospital for my infusion, I was swept up into a group hug from the nurses who had been in touch with me the day after the hurricane and were aware of our situation. They also told me about the ordeal through which Patsy and his wife had gone. Patsy's wife was in poor health just as Patsy was. I think like most people they didn't want to be an inconvenience to anyone. They went to bed a few hours before the hurricane hit, and Patsy had woken up because he heard a noise. He walked out of his bedroom to find his house filling with water. Patsy was not a healthy man, and his illnesses took away his physical strength. He used a walker and was in constant pain. Somehow, as the water in their house rose, that amazing man was able to help his wife up attic steps and into the attic where they would be safe. 9-1-1 notified Patsy that someone would try to get to them—they just weren't sure when it would happen given how bad the flooding was. Patsy went back down the attic steps to try and grab bottles of water and forgot his cellphone was in his pocket. The water ruined his phone, cutting them off from the outside world. He made it back into the attic, now without any means to make phone calls. He and his wife remained in the attic until a boat rescued them by pulling up to their dock, two days after the hurricane destroyed his home. The boat transported them to a safe area where ambulances were waiting. They were both hospitalized.

When I learned of their ordeal, I kept trying to leave voicemails for him, even though I knew his phone wasn't working. I didn't have any idea which hospital he was in, and due to H.I.P.A.A. laws, the nurses couldn't reveal anything else to me regarding his health, other than letting me know he was safe. A few days went by, and Patsy had his phone replaced, and he was released from the hospital. He contacted me, and we spoke for over an hour. I was so thankful he and his wife had survived, but I felt so distressed at their situation because I couldn't help them. I was in the midst of my own mess. The hurricane ruined their home just as our home was, only much worse. Where we were able to salvage some things, all of Patsy's stuff was completely gone.

Patsy and his wife couldn't move in with either of his sons because both homes had staircases and neither he nor his wife would be able to manage them. They were desperate and were lucky enough to find an apartment in an independent living facility a few towns away. They had to scramble to buy furniture and clothing and replace everything they owned. The good news was that they were alive and had a place to live. The bad news was that due to his new address, his treatments would be at a different hospital and we would no longer have our infusions together. We both loved our friendship and conversations so much that we made a pact to find the time in the midst of our chaotic lives to keep up with phone calls. The hurricane and how it affected us was just one more thing we had in common. It was so interesting that the hurricane was the cause of us not being together for our infusions anymore, yet it was also the thing that strengthened and solidified our bond even more.

Three days after the hurricane marked Oliver's second birthday. While we were struggling with the chaos of the storm and worrying about my ovary, we didn't want his birthday to be forgotten. It's silly to think Oliver knew what a "birthday" even was and clearly, we needed to do something to take our minds off of everything, so we took Oliver to Petco and splurged on some new toys and treats. Unfortunately, the store had a recent remodel, and our weird bulldog decided he didn't like the set-up of the new fixtures, and for some odd reason, refused to walk beyond the front doors. Poor Oliver and his quirkiness. It didn't stop him from getting the love and attention he needed; the employees came to him to pet him as he stood, semi-frozen, at the front door. Everyone laughed at how strange it was that he refused to walk into the remodeled store. I laughed along with them on the outside, but on the inside, I was wondering if his insurance would cover a doggy psychiatrist. Could it be that our sudden displacement and a newly remodeled pet store was just too much for Oliver's little brain to handle?

Along with Oliver's second birthday came a vet visit for some vaccinations. As usual, everyone fawned over Oliver, and he ate it up. Apparently, hurricanes, attention, and love make you gain weight because when they lifted him onto the scale, our two-year-old weighed seventy fucking pounds. Jimmy and I were both embarrassed. Being around him every day, we didn't realize how big he was getting. Dr. Denyer gently reminded us that carrying extra weight wasn't good for Oliver. They took some measurements and were able to tell us how much, based on his age and measurements, he should weigh. And that number was far away from seventy pounds. Oliver needed to lose close to twenty pounds and because we wanted him to live a long, healthy life we agreed to do our best to get him to move more and try to lose the weight naturally before putting him on a prescription diet.

While my mind juggled Oliver's weight issues, the damage on our house, and dealing with the insurance company and F.E.M.A., I still had a black cloud of worry hanging over my head regarding the tests I needed to have done on my ovary. If I could have punched that ovary, I would have. For real. I was no longer of child-bearing age so why the fuck did this stupid thing have to cause me issues now? Couldn't it have waited, oh I don't know, until after we rebuilt our house and replaced our belongings? Stupid ovary. Finally, a little over a week after the hurricane, I was able to get in touch with my gynecologist, pick up the prescription and have the tests I needed. The results of my test came just as our F.E.M.A. assessor showed up to do a walkthrough of our property and its damage. As he walked around our soggy mess of a house with his clipboard, tallying up the dollar amount of damage, my phone rang, and the doctor told me my ovary was clear! I started crying both from relief but also because I knew our insurance was only going to cover about half of the amount of damage. I'm pretty sure our F.E.M.A assessor thought I was a lunatic. And I didn't mind because I was a lunatic with a healthy ovary.

As the first couple of weeks after the hurricane passed by, I was overwhelmed by the offers of help we received, oddly enough from many former classmates (thanks, Facebook!) I hadn't seen in years. Some offered help with cleaning and gutting the house. Others offered an ear if I needed to vent. It was humbling and also embarrassing. I am never one to ask for any help. I think that is because I would rather be the person helping than the person asking for help. It's not that I am above asking for help; it's more about being a control freak. Face it, when someone is giving you their help, you are sort of at their mercy. It would be like asking someone to fold my laundry and then having to smile and say, "thank you"— when it's clearly folded all wrong, not color coded and the tags are visible. How could I ever ask for help when I want things to be a specific way? Silly, I know.

The hurricane left me without any choice but to take the help people offered us. From needing a place to live, to contractors to starting work on our house without being paid yet, to my dad breaking his back to help clean up the debris—these were all forms of help we needed and received. And it was humbling. Some people dropped what they were doing to help us move out the belongings we were able to save, while others called to say they were sorry for what had happened. And as humbled as I was by those willing to help, I was equally as hurt and angry by expecting help from people who didn't offer to help at all. It's an odd dichotomy, feeling the overwhelming love from people you'd never expect it from, while also to trying to work through the hurt caused by friends and family not quite understanding the loss with which you are dealing.

We also had many calls from family and friends where they expressed compassion for what we were going through and would usually tack on an offer of some sort, like getting together for dinner or a night out. Sadly, out of the many offers we received, only one couple followed through with it and had us over one night for cake and coffee, and some much-needed conversation that didn't contain the words, "F.E.M.A., insurance, or hurricane" in it. I learned through this experience that some people could only make a general offer to show some support and they just didn't have it in them to follow up. People with good intentions will offer to take your mind off of things; people with good character will follow through. I feel like more people need to have integrity and mean what they say. It took me some time, but I now practice every day to use only the words I truly mean. For example, if I ask you how you are, it isn't because it's the segue to another topic or just a weird version of saying hello. I do want to know HOW. YOU. ARE. That one night of meeting with two other couples and enjoying a few laughs meant everything to us. I guess we have Oliver to thank for that since it was our friends from the dog park, Ray and Kathy (Callie's owners) and Patty and Tony (Anton's owners), who took the time to boost us up emotionally when we needed it.

Struggling with the mix of emotions Hurricane Sandy brought me wasn't easy. On top of what we were dealing with personally, I felt a pang of sadness for my friends and neighbors who suffered through the storm also. It was strange to know that on our small stretch of road, our house sat the slightest bit lower than the houses surrounding us. Those houses remained mostly unscathed. It is very easy to fall into a "why me" mentality and fill your soul with self-pity. Our immediate neighbors might not have been displaced or suffered the loss of material possessions on the same level we did, but they suffered without electricity for thirteen days. That meant no heat during some cold days and nights. I felt obligated to check in on them each day I came to our house to shovel debris or sop up water. Standing in the middle of a house that was wet, sandy and muddy, made it easy for me to cry and ask over and over again, "WHY US? WHY DID THIS HAPPEN TO US?" Then I would clear my head, remember that I had heat, lights, and hot water at my parents' house; many people in our community did not.

The next several weeks passed in a blur of F.E.M.A. representatives, police checkpoints in our neighborhood, and insurance phone calls that lasted for hours. There were many tears, lots of frustration, panic attacks, and many sleepless nights. We were so grateful to have a place to live, and we were so thankful my parents didn't even hesitate to help us. Trying to make things work living together, however, was frustrating for all of us—except for Oliver. All he knew was that we were now at his grandparent's house and he was totally cool with it. He no longer had a crate, only a comfy dog bed to sleep on and he made the adjustment just fine, relishing in all of the attention he was receiving in his temporary home. It helped that we kept a big supply of bones and new toys for him. He never once looked at me to question why we were now sleeping at Grandma and Grandpa's house. We kept his routine the same as much as possible—I would spend a few hours working at our house and then make the twenty-minute drive back to my parents' just to feed him, take him to the bathroom and a short walk, then drive back to our house to work some more. I would do the drive back and forth several times a day, trying my best to not inconvenience my Mom by asking her to help with Oliver. Oliver wasn't confused or upset or hurt or angry over our misfortune. Oliver took the love and affection he was receiving and thought, "BONUS!"

Oliver adapted way better than the rest of us did to his new home. From timing when to take showers to learning how my Dad likes the forks to go a certain way in the dishwasher, it was a big adjustment for us four humans. Oliver was happy he now had four sets of hands to pet him and scratch his butt. While his daily trips to the park stopped, we did still bring him there on Sundays, the one day we all "took a day off" from working on the house. Being away from his dog friends all week, Oliver found a new appreciation for them. He was sweeter, kinder, and only ruined half the amount of other dogs' toys that he usually destroyed. Keeping a routine for Oliver also helped me stay a little calmer. Going for a short walk with him around my parents' neighborhood allowed me to decompress and take a few moments to appreciate how lucky we were and work through the disappointment I felt from not getting the help I had expected.

I knew, logically, that when I help people, it is because I want to—not because I am expecting something in return. Expecting something in return, in my mind, is a transaction. But logic aside, I was upset by those who didn't help or even offer to help without the intention of actually doing so. I would walk around my parents' neighborhood with Oliver and think about all of these things. Why do we layer expectations onto our relationships? I didn't want to be one of those people who keeps a mental tally of the things I did to help people so that I could throw it in their faces when they failed me when I needed them. These emotions are heavy shit to stir up when you're in the thick of your life being in upheaval. It was important to me to see through my personal pain and understand that it was so wrong of me to assume people weren't helping because they didn't want to. If people can help and will help, it is because they want to. If they can't help or don't want to, I knew I could not take it personally. People will help or they won't. There isn't anything that should be attached or come after that. They will. Or they won't. I needed to let go of the hurt and those expectations that I applied to relationships. We had a roof over our heads, we were safe, and Oliver was happy. Oliver wasn't able to determine if someone *should have* come to scratch his butt; he was just grateful for those who did. I needed to be grateful for the positives that were floating to the surface of the cesspool of emotions that Hurricane Sandy caused.

And if Oliver was the "Prince of Silverton," he was the "King of Holiday City." We met so many of my parents' neighbors in their retirement community, all because everyone would come to see Oliver as he sat on their front lawn. It was a hysterical sight: dozens of senior citizens walking across streets and down sidewalks, just to come pet Oliver and have some conversation. We met people my parents didn't even know! Oliver attracted people like a magnet. He had his favorites—a couple named Harry and Jan Giesel—who lived three houses away from my parents. Harry and Jan had a dog of their own and were what we call "dog people"—people who love dogs so much they cannot see one without stopping and petting it. Oliver won them over with his full body wiggle, despite their dog not being too fond of him. Harry and Jan were so kind to Oliver. They were always ready to give him love and attention and even baked him homemade treats at Christmas time! Seeing Oliver so happy, giving just as much love to the people in the neighborhood as they gave to him, was fascinating. Sure, he was a sucker for attention, but every single person that walked over to see Oliver sitting on that front lawn left with a huge smile on his or her face. He brought joy and happiness to people, and the entire neighborhood grew to love him.

What Oliver Taught Me: Listen, life can take some shitty turns. If I am to believe it all happens for a reason, then I have to believe the bad things have a reason, too. We can't always pick and chose what happens. There will always be good times and always be not-so-good times. We must believe each situation happens for a reason, even when it's hard to understand why. And despite being displaced, losing a lot of material possessions, and the stress Hurricane Sandy caused, Oliver taught me to be grateful for the love and help we did receive. He absorbed every hug he was given and gave that love right back, tenfold. He relished in every "hello" someone gave him in his temporary neighborhood.

During this trying and stressful time, I also was reminded that we give because we want to, not because we have to and when we give, it should be unconditional. For me to put expectations on family or friends who I felt should have helped us, was selfish. Keeping mental tallies of who helped and who didn't, is even more ridiculous. I have done my best since this challenging time to choose and use my words with care. If I say I am going to "be there" for someone, I will be there in every way possible whether it is physically, emotionally, or just a pair of ears that know how to listen. Our words need to have meaning and intent.

I realized I needed to learn to be appreciative of those who showed up for us, literally and figuratively. And now I make sure I show up for my friends who need help, too. I want people to walk away from me with a smile, just like our new, temporary neighbors did with Oliver.

chapter
EIGHT

January 2013 came, and we were still out of our house due to Hurricane Sandy. We did our best to stay focused on getting back into our home as quickly as possible. My Dad, who had been buying houses and renovating them for resale for many years, along with contractors, subcontractors, Jimmy and myself, all worked endlessly to keep progress rolling. And thankfully, we only experienced a few hiccups along the way. I look back now at this time in our lives and while we had help from people physically, what kept us lifted emotionally was Oliver. It didn't matter how bad things were; Oliver only had to give us a body wiggle, and it would make us smile.

That is not to say that things were perfect in Oliver's world. While he adapted to his new living situation and attention from many new neighbors, his regurgitation returned—all over my parents' carpets. Thankfully, due to both of them having horrible hearing (sorry, Mom and Dad, but it's true), there were many times I would be awake in the middle of the night doing laundry and cleaning carpets because Oliver would regurgitate all over—and they would never even know. There was one particular day when I brought Oliver inside from a walk, and he proceeded to have what is now referred to in hushed tones as Puke Fest 2013. There wasn't one surface of my parents' living room that Oliver didn't anoint with regurgitation. None of this ever bothered Oliver. He would regurgitate and then give a little wiggle and be ready to play or eat or go for a walk. It was a total embarrassment for me. It's bad enough when you have a dog with these gastrointestinal issues in your home. It's a million times worse when it's not only someone else's home but someone who had kindly taken you in when you needed a place to live. Back to the vet we went and finally, FINALLY, a switch in food, realizations of some new food intolerances along with some daily Pepcid, and things improved as far as stopping Oliver's regurgitation issues. As thrilled as we were for the remedy of the regurgitation issues, we were reminded once again how heavy he was when it took two vet technicians to lift his fat ass onto the scale. We set a deadline to try and have him lose some weight. Unfortunately, Oliver was super lazy, so it was almost inevitable a prescription diet was in his future.

Once the contractors gutted our house and the rebuilding of floors and walls began, it was as though we could finally see the light at the end of the tunnel. We considered ourselves very lucky that our insurance company worked quickly and efficiently to process our claims. The horror stories we heard from other people affected by the hurricane were awful—the biggest complaint seemingly how delayed the processing of claims were. We were so fortunate to have my parents. They would pay out of their own pockets for materials and labor, and once the insurance company reimbursed us in installments, we would reimburse my Mom and Dad. If not for my parents fronting us tens of thousands of dollars, the progress of rebuilding our house would have taken well over a year. The F.E.M.A. assessor estimated our damages at around $110,000, and our insurance only covered $59,000 of that. If not for my Dad doing the work our insurance didn't cover himself, we probably would have had to walk away from our home like many people in our neighborhood had to do.

The magnitude of what we lost was still astounding as we would shop to replace necessities. I not only learned where our local home improvement store stocked every single item in their stores, but I also had many nervous breakdowns in some of those aisles. I began to give myself pep talks before walking into these stores. "I WILL FIND THAT GROUT! THEY WILL HAVE OUR HEAT VENTS IN STOCK! THIS TIME, THEY WILL MIX THE RIGHT COLOR PAINT FOR OUR WALLS, SO WE DON'T HAVE TO PAINT IT FOR A THIRD TIME!" These pep talks carried me through shopping in stores where I was out of my element, and as I learned more about how one rebuilds a house, I felt powerful walking down the aisles thinking, "I know what fucking tongue and groove flooring is!"

Small victories came in things we could salvage: canned food, bedding that I had stored on upper shelves of closets, and a few things in our bathroom medicine cabinet. All of these small things added up, and we were so very grateful to have saved them. I was so overwhelmed with thinking about every item we had taken for granted that we now had to replace. I cried hysterically while buying a new hamper. I had a panic attack when trying to pick out new silverware. I was brought to tears because I had to replace condiments. As silly as it sounds, having that old bottle of ketchup or mustard in your refrigerator well beyond its expiration date is a luxury!

One day, near the end of January 2013, I drove over to check on the progress of the house. Things had improved, and we were now at a point where each visit to the house made us excited that we were so much closer to moving back home. On this particular day, almost all of the walls were being built, and sheetrock was going up. A contractor had subcontracted the job of rebuilding the walls in the house. That subcontractor brought in, unbeknownst to us at the time, what is known as day laborers to replace the sheetrock. Day laborers were common throughout all of the towns hit by Hurricane Sandy, due to the immense amount of work being done and the shortage of hands to do it. The subcontractor picked up some day laborers from a designated zone in a neighboring town. Most of the guys being picked up were paid in cash for a day or two's worth of work before moving on to a new job. While the concept of day laborers made complete sense, it also meant if a job wasn't done correctly or sufficiently, the chances of tracking down those particular workers could prove difficult.

All I was concerned with was seeing some real walls in our bare bones of a house, so when I walked into my front door, I was ecstatic to see what looked like individual rooms instead of beams everywhere. I introduced myself to the guy that was replacing the sheetrock in one of our spare bedrooms, and he indicated he didn't speak English but told me his name was Pablo. I was so excited to see actual walls again instead of just beams and studs, and since we had a language barrier between us, I tried to high-five him to show my enthusiasm. He shook his head "no." I wasn't sure if he didn't understand what I was trying to do, or if he just was letting me know he wouldn't stoop down to my geeky level with a high-five. Instead, I gave him a thumbs up sign as a way to indicate my excitement and gratitude, and he smiled. I left the house knowing that by the very next day, we would have walls again, which meant we were one GIANT step closer to moving back home. I was giddy for the first time since the hurricane and could allow myself to start visualizing how we would be living in our home again. I tried not to stress too much about all of the furniture and essentials that we still needed to replace.

I returned to our house the next day to admire the new sheetrock, and I was so happy to see all rooms had walls—actual walls! I brought with me some items, such as clothing that would hang in the closets, and was excited to start filling up the house with pieces of us again. I opened up a closet to start unpacking, and my jaw hit the floor. It was empty. I was extremely confused for a few minutes. I began checking each location where we had placed salvaged items—they were all gone. Cans of soup and food, old medications, sheets and pillowcases, blankets, Jimmy's cologne, a toaster oven, a Jack LaLane Juicer—GONE. Someone had taken it ALL. My first reaction was to start crying hysterically. I couldn't understand how anyone could physically see with their own fucking eyeballs the devastation we were trying to dig ourselves out of and still decide to steal what little we had managed to salvage. At that moment, while I didn't know who had taken it, I knew there was only one person who had access to the house in the past twenty-four hours: the sheetrock guy. I was furious and sad and hurt and had we not had sparkling new sheetrock on the walls I might have punched some holes in all of them. I gave the guy a fucking thumbs up! I wasted a thumbs up on a possible thief! We shared a symbolic sign of excitement and gratitude! WHAT. THE. FUCK.

I called Jimmy at work and began screaming that someone stole the belongings we had saved. I didn't know what to do since we had no proof. Contacting the subcontractor would have been useless. I was angry, hurt, sad, and disappointed. People can tell you, "Oh, those are just things! You can replace things!" I want to punch those people in their throats. Yes, I know they are just things. But they were things we salvaged from a goddamn hurricane. A HURRICANE.

It took me about two days to get over feeling angry. I wanted to—and needed to—somehow put a positive spin on this or I was seriously going to end up in a padded cell, rocking back and forth while muttering about stolen soup. I convinced myself that maybe whoever took those things needed them desperately. Maybe they needed to feed their family my cans of soup. Maybe they needed to put sheets and pillowcases on their beds. Maybe they needed my four-year-old antibiotics to stop the pain from an infected tooth. And maybe they needed Jimmy's cologne so they could smell fantastic while heating up my soup and swallowing my old meds. Okay, so I'm not perfect, and a little anger would slip in here and there. But, for my own sanity, I needed to believe someone stole our shit because they needed it more than we needed it. So, that's how I thought about it, and that line of thinking got me through those days of feeling lower than low.

I had—and still have moments—where I lose faith in humanity because of that situation even though so much time has passed. For all of the good people who helped us, that one terrible blow almost erased all of the good. It made me wonder why the negatives in life weigh so much more than the positives. If someone smiles at you, you probably don't even make a mental note of it. But, I am willing to bet if someone walked by and gave you a look of disgust, you'd make a note of it and think about it. I had to—and still have to—force myself not to allow that one act outweigh the good that others had done during such an emotional and stressful time. It takes work to change your thinking, and it takes more work to let the good outweigh the bad.

Our lives were moving forward. Specialists did their mold treatments; vapor barriers were in place; we painted the walls and ceilings. My Dad installed our cabinets, bathroom tiles, wood floors, kitchen backsplash, and closet doors with help from both Jimmy and myself. Professionals installed our countertops as one of the final projects. We were getting closer to being able to move back home, and we were happy. Each day that I drove to my house with my car filled with items that were able to be moved in, I reminded myself how lucky we were as I drove past the vacant lots in my neighborhood where houses once stood. So many people were affected much worse than we were, and it was sad to see many people simply walking away from their homes because there wasn't any way for them to rebuild. I won't comment on the politics of it all, but I will say this: Not enough was done after the hurricane to help the people who needed it the most. The government did not do all that it should have done. It was disappointing. My heart ached for so many people whose lives were torn apart by not only a natural disaster but also by a government that failed them. So many people walked away from this disaster having to start over. That is not okay.

Throughout this rebuilding process, Patsy and I kept in constant contact. He was one of the people whom the government failed. The red tape buried Patsy and his wife in a never-ending sea of bureaucracy. All they wanted was to return home but every step of the way, Patsy suffered a setback due to the government. The claims he filed were unable to be processed by the appropriate sources because he didn't file them under the first name on his birth certificate, despite showing every form of identification known to man. Each time Patsy thought he had made a little progress, something would go wrong, and he would learn he would be out of his house for longer than he ever thought he would. He also suffered some physical setbacks and was in and out of the hospital several times. Each time, I would visit him, and my heart would break a little more. He had been through so much in his life. With the hurricane, being displaced, and all of the loss he and his wife suffered, seeing him sick in the hospital helped me appreciate life a little more. Since we no longer had our treatments together, visiting him those times always made me feel better because we had that genuine friendship most of us long for in life—but rarely see. We commiserated over the hurricane and realized this was just one more bond we had between us.

Patsy was so proud of his time in the Navy and one year prior, for Christmas I had a mug made for him with the name of the Destroyer on which he was stationed. He told me that when his sons were cleaning up debris, one of the handfuls of items the hurricane didn't destroy was that mug. It made us both smile, and that mug came to represent the resilience Patsy had in life. He did, however, lose his very favorite thing—his baseball hat that had his Destroyer logo on it. It was part of Patsy's signature look: a cardigan, his wallet in his sock, cell phone by his side and his "USS Bristol DD-857" baseball hat. I remember times when the hospital admitted Patsy, and I'd visit him, and he always looked so different to me without that hat. More vulnerable, perhaps. That hat invoked such pride in him that I knew when he would eventually move back into his home as he vowed to do, and our treatments would be together again, I would replace that hat for him.

I continued restocking our house with necessities and food as each room became complete again. As weird as it sounds, I felt as if I needed to have the house one hundred percent complete so when we moved back in, the transition would be seamless for Oliver. Jimmy and I didn't matter; Oliver did. Despite how well he adapted to the recent changes in his life, I wanted Oliver to walk in our front door to a home that, while it looked different and was decorated differently with new floors and carpeting, he would love and feel comfortable in it. Dog beds were purchased and laid down. I placed toys and bones in the same spots where we had kept them before the hurricane. New area rugs went down in the spots where our old rugs once laid. As we U-Hauled our belongings back to our home and unpacked, I made sure everything was in its place so that Oliver wasn't walking into chaos when we brought him home the next day.

We needed to acknowledge the love and kindness my parents showed us by giving us a place to live and the inconvenience of having two more people and a dog in their home. We also wanted to express our thanks for all of the help my dad gave us in rebuilding and fronting us the money to keep the progress going until the insurance company reimbursed us. The words "thank you" wasn't enough. We purchased them some gift cards for dinner, but there wasn't anything—words or gifts—that could ever show them how grateful we were. It wasn't always easy for any of us, but we made it through.

Finally on Tuesday, February 12, 2013, we moved back home! We weren't sure how Oliver would react considering every square inch of the house had been rebuilt, repaired, remodeled and redecorated. He hadn't been back to the house since the day we evacuated, October 29, 2012. I did my best impression of a proud soccer mom and had my phone ready to record his reaction. When he got out of the car, Oliver ran like a lunatic to the front door, jumped inside and ran into every single room. He explored the whole house, his body wiggling the entire time. As I recorded the experience, all I could think was that this chubby, sweet, boy never knew why we left our home or what had happened. He didn't know what we had lost. All he knew was that he was HOME. Sure, everything looked and smelled different since he had last been home, but he was so happy. It was the best feeling so see him thrilled to be back home.

He slept well on that first night, and by the second day, Oliver resumed his life right where he left off in October. He didn't forget where his favorite spot was in the backyard to sun himself. He didn't forget where his food and water bowls belonged. The surroundings and material things had all changed, but our routines and the love we shared were still there. Oliver spent that first full day back home doing his favorite things: eating, pooping, sleeping and sunning himself on the back step. He had missed the freedom of being off-leash in a big fenced-in yard while living with my parents. He sniffed around and was curious as to why there wasn't any grass, trees, or shrubs, but none of it bothered him one bit. He finished his first full day back home by stepping in his poop, something he hadn't done in ages. We were home again—literally and figuratively.

The hurricane and how it impacted us was a long, exhausting, and trying journey. We took a cue from Oliver and began to enjoy being home again, tried not to focus on the things we had lost and did our best to look ahead to our future.

What Oliver Taught Me: There were moments during the aftermath of Hurricane Sandy when I wished I could be privy to only the positive things it brought out, like watching people help each other. It was frustrating to have to see the bad—like, people looting—along with the good. However, seeing those disappointing incidents helped me appreciate the good ones even more.

Oliver didn't know the magnitude of what we had lost; he only knew he had gained two extra people to love him twenty-four hours a day by moving in with my parents. And, that he had a new neighborhood to explore and new friends to meet. Each moment I spent with Oliver during the breaks when we weren't working on the house gave me small bursts of insight. As we went for our walks in our temporary 'hood, I realized I needed to be more like Oliver and allow people to help us, love us, and lift us up. I needed to absorb the good with complete gratitude that the bad shit couldn't tarnish.

Oliver met so many new friends during the stay with my parents, but he never expected them to love him. Maybe he had hoped for a few extra butt scratches, but the amount of love he received was pure joy for him. I realized I couldn't live my life any longer placing expectations on people. I shouldn't base relationships on expectations. This lesson was an important one to learn and seeing Oliver accept life and love for what it is, helped me to do the same.

chapter
NINE

As 2013 marched on, we became more active with a local bulldog rescue—the MidAtlantic Bulldog Rescue (MABDR). I had come across MABDR after seeing my Instagram friends posting about fundraisers a few years prior, and while we had attended one of them, I started learning more about the rescue through some of the volunteers and the founder, Cathy Kittell. Even though Oliver wasn't a rescue, we were so happy to learn what Cathy, and the volunteers were doing to help bulldogs in need. Bulldogs are such a wonderful breed, and people fall quickly in love with the idea of having one and can easily be enamored enough to bring a bully home without truly knowing what it entails. English bulldogs are prone to many medical issues, as you can tell just by reading about Winnie and Oliver. Sometimes, several medical issues can arise at once which in turn, causes high vet bills. Not everyone can take on that expense and sadly, many people end up surrendering their bulldogs because they are then facing financial difficulties they weren't expecting. People like Cathy Kittell and her volunteers are the light at the end of the tunnel for most of these dogs who then need new homes.

As I got to know Cathy and learned more about MABDR, I wanted to do more to help. There is so much that goes into rescuing and rehoming a bulldog; Cathy is an angel for all of the work she does. From transporting bulldogs to having them evaluated medically, to taking care of surgeries and illnesses, to placing them with the right foster families and then eventually, finding them their forever homes—MABDR does it all. Coordinating all of these things isn't any small feat, but Cathy is so good at what she does, she makes it seem easy. The more I learned about MABDR, the more I wanted to help in some way. While fostering wasn't an option for us since we had our hands full with Oliver, especially given his medical issues, we did the best we could by sending in donations and attending the fundraisers. These events not only raise money for the rescue but they allow people like us—insane bulldog freaks—to get to meet other like-minded weirdos. You have never experienced true love until you are in the middle of a hundred slobbering bulldogs. It's a massive amount of snorting, wiggling, and vying for attention. And that is just the humans fawning all over the bulldogs.

Through the fundraisers, we met so many fantastic people and their bulldogs. These social events where our bulldogs were welcome were also an excellent place to meet up with our Instagram friends. Let's face it; you never want to meet a random stranger you know from the internet in a park all by yourself. So, all of us New Jersey bulldog freaks would arrange to meet at MABDR's fundraisers. Say what you will about social media, but the one thing that it clearly does is unite all of us kooky bulldog lovers. There's a million of us out there, all willing to share our quirky bulldogs with the world. Oliver was so happy each time we went to the Bully Bash and Bullypaloolza fundraisers, which happened twice a year. For one of the events, we were thrilled when his sister, Henrietta and her Mom, Laura, could meet us. Oliver and Henrietta had only gotten together twice since being separated from each other: one time at the Alvarez's house and one time at our house. Henrietta dominated Oliver both times, despite being half his weight, however, at our house, she sensed it was his domain, and she was a little shyer. We were interested to see how they would behave on neutral territory.

During this particular event, Oliver and Henrietta spotted each other before any of us humans spotted each other. They ran up to each other's faces as if to say hello, and then stood side-by-side, leaning into each other. Of course, all of us started taking pictures. To this day, when I see those pictures, I haven't any doubt in my mind that dogs remember their siblings because Oliver didn't behave the way he would with any other dog. It was different; there was love on a different level. Gone was the competitive nature these two had previously had. Henrietta didn't dominate Oliver, nor did he try to dominate her. It was pure love and maybe a little bit of, "Hey, this is SO crazy! Look at all of these bulldogs! WTF is this place? Thank God we know each other because I don't know any of these other crazy bastards! Oh wait, there is Chunk. I know him!" The pictures from that moment are priceless. Sadly, we knew it would most likely be the last time we would all get together as Henrietta and the Alvarez family were leaving New Jersey and moving to Florida.

Not only did Jimmy and I enjoy going to the MABDR fundraisers, but we felt that in the future, adopting a rescue would be a great thing for us to do. We wanted to learn as much as we could about MABDR and get to know Cathy and the volunteers involved. If anyone in this world has a golden heart, it is the person who can take on coordinating and running a dog rescue. Cathy isn't any exception to that rule. I knew at some point, in some way, I would love to help her more, but I wasn't sure if we could take on a rescue dog. It's a warped way of thinking—knowing a rescue dog needs a home, but being so empathetic to its suffering, that is unbearable to erase what it has gone through your mind and only think about giving a dog a fresh start. Does a dog think of you as its savior, or did it only believe that you were taking it away from the only home it has ever known? Maybe I'm the only lunatic who wonders about those things? But, I have seen firsthand how dogs that are rescued show appreciation to their new owners.

When attending the fundraisers, I always had a fear of people thinking less of us because we purchased Oliver from a breeder. I realize that is my insecurity; rescue or not, giving a bulldog a solid, stable home filled with love is the goal. And honestly, before finding Oliver's breeders, we had applied to be fosters or adoptive parents with a different well-known New Jersey rescue and were never contacted by them, despite meeting all requirements, giving a donation (which they asked for), and having previous bulldog experience. That had soured us a little, especially when the rescue was pushing so hard for donations and advertising bulldogs they needed to place. What we learned about MABDR was the complete opposite of this other rescue, and after getting to know Cathy and becoming friends with her and some of her volunteers, I felt such relief that not all rescues run in the same manner despite having the same goals at heart.

We attended as many MABDR fundraising events as we could because it was such a source of joy for us—and Oliver, too. For one event, in particular, we had t-shirts made that said, "Oliver's Mom" and "Oliver's Dad." Our choice of clothing would have mortified Oliver if he was human. Shit, he wasn't human and was still probably embarrassed. (But this was a two-way street. How did we know *he* wouldn't embarrass *us* by stepping in his own shit in front of everyone?) We did this so we would be easy to identify for new Instagram and Facebook friends we had yet to meet in-person. It's hard to figure out who is who when there are so many people. The Wonder Bar in Asbury Park hosts these events, and there is a beautiful outdoor deck where dogs are welcome. As we walked through the gates of the Wonder Bar, I had a moment of panic where all that was flashing across my brain was, "HOLY SHIT, WE

LOOK LIKE IDIOTS WEARING THESE SHIRTS," but that quickly dissipated as so many of our Instagram friends walked up and introduced themselves. It took meeting new people to a new, lazy level.

Life was chugging along, and Oliver was doing well until January of 2014 when he had reached a point of fatness that was no longer acceptable. He was still holding steady at seventy pounds, despite our efforts to have him lose weight. Dr. Denyer suggested he begin a prescription diet food. His measurements were taken once again and calculated, and we were astonished to learn that ideally, Oliver should weigh around forty-five pounds. Both Jimmy and I couldn't ever see him losing *that* much weight. He'd look like a skeleton with a gigantic head! Dr. Denyer suggested we shoot for around fifty pounds. His diet was to be a long, slow weight loss process and despite how cute His Royal Chubbiness looked, we knew it was for Oliver's best health that he lose a few pounds. Aside from the weight issues, Oliver was doing great! His leg had healed, his regurgitation was under control, he was back to playing at the park, and Oliver became the calm, lazy, sweet bulldog we never thought he'd be after experiencing how awful he was as a puppy. It was such a miraculous thing; I heard angels singing every time I looked down with pride at my lovable weirdo.

He did develop a few new quirks which were very curious. Since renovating the house after the hurricane, we changed the color of our hardwood flooring throughout the house from a walnut color to a darker cherry color. This new cherry color was the bane of Oliver's existence. It was extra shiny, and in some areas where there were particularly bright reflections in the floor from lights and windows, Oliver became too afraid to walk. He would stand for a minute, trying to work up the courage to move and then would run as fast as he could over the cursed spots, which usually ended with his legs coming out from under him. Since he already had one knee surgery, and since a dog psychiatrist was too expensive, I had to buy random area rugs to place over the troublesome spots. There was one particular spot in our living where an area rug was simply not going to go, or my OCD mind would explode. I figured Oliver would just have to adapt to the cherry-colored floor in that area. Oliver's solution? When he reached that spot on the floor, he would turn his stocky body around and would walk backward. My dog was *moonwalking*. Like Michael Jackson. *Across our living room floor.* It was both hysterical and disturbing. We figured in time he would outgrow this weird fear. He never did. And thank goodness for that. Since Oliver rarely moved faster than a snail's pace, I could never take videos of him. But now, the worlds of Facebook and Instagram were lit up with #Oliverthemoonwalkingbulldog! (Go ahead, search Instagram. It's real.) It was unbelievable to me that Oliver could be dumb enough to be afraid of flooring, yet smart enough to figure a way around it.

While Oliver was thriving and moonwalking, I was deteriorating. My Crohn's was becoming even more out-of-control, and my infusions weren't helping me at all. After having some tests done, my doctor determined that being on Remicade for the last eight years, I had built up too many antibodies for the drug to be effective. Since every medication before Remicade hadn't helped me at all, I was clinging to the minuscule amount of relief I would feel immediately after each infusion. But as each day after an infusion passed, my symptoms became worse. My doctor felt it was time to change to a different immunosuppressive drug, but I refused. After each treatment, I would have two or three days where I felt a little better. Holding on to those two or three days seemed more important to me than throwing them away and trying a new drug that might not help me at all. While discussing options with my doctor, I learned that if I were to go off of Remicade and a new medication didn't help me there wasn't any chance of going back to Remicade. As someone who always needs a safety net of sorts, I felt as though changing medications was more of a risk than a possible benefit. While my doctor didn't push me, he did present me with the options I could have once I was willing to step out of my comfort zone and try something new.

Realistically, I knew I needed to change medications. If we live a life worried about what might not happen, we close ourselves off to the possibilities of the great things that *can* happen. I had grown so accustomed to living a fraction of life, that I convinced myself it was okay to live this way. It wasn't okay, and while it took me a few more years to realize that, I stood firm about not making any changes. Each time I would see my gastroenterologist, he would gently remind me there were other options we could try but would also say that he, too, was afraid to make any changes. This relationship between patient and doctor served me well; he wasn't pressuring me to take a huge risk even though we both knew it was time. Ultimately, my life and health are up to me so I can never fault him for any of it. But, when I look back at just how much I was letting Crohn's control my life, I am sad I wasn't willing to listen more and take some risks. Change is scary, and a possible regression in my disease worried me too much to make a change.

Over the next several months as winter of 2014 blended into spring, Oliver was responding very well to his new diet and successfully shedding some of the extra pounds he was carrying. With each visit to Dr. Denyer to weigh Oliver, Jimmy and I would place bets on how much we thought he weighed. It was so odd to see the number on the scale go down yet, being with Oliver for every waking moment of the day, we didn't necessarily notice his weight loss. Other people did notice, however, and commented how great he looked. And I could tell he felt good, too. He wanted to go for more walks, and he seemed to be more energetic, even though he still felt the need to rest his head on any object that came near it, as though that big noggin of his weighed sixty pounds. At least one of us was doing well.

There were days when I would stare at Oliver and wish I could be more like him. I know, I know—that's a fucking weird thing to say, especially since stepping in my poop isn't exactly something I'd enjoy. But Oliver was entirely okay with making changes. His new prescription diet food was the BOMB as far as he was concerned. He loved it and began behaving like a bucking bronco whenever he knew it was time to eat, throwing his body into the air with excitement to consume, frankly, something that looked and smelled disgusting. It was interesting for me to look into our situations deeper: Oliver didn't have a choice. He ate what we gave him to better his health. And he loved it, embraced it, and thrived. I had the option to change medications to better *my* health, and I chose not to change. By exercising that choice, I opted to live a diminished, unhappy life where shitting my pants was something that happened every so often. Who would make that kind of a choice? Me. Because I'm an idiot. Go ahead and say it, because I know you're thinking it. And sadly, it took me a few more years to GET IT.

Scenarios of what could happen negatively filled my life instead of the possibilities and hope of the positive things that might occur. I'm not a risk-taker and playing Russian roulette with medications and all of their side effects and whether or not they would cause me any setbacks with Crohn's wasn't my idea of an exciting, new adventure. Giving up my Remade infusions would mean giving up feeling semi-okay for three days out of the week. Somewhere along the years, I had become someone who wasn't seeing the glass as half full, but rather as the glass having a crack in it and as long as I kept my thumb over the crack, the contents might not leak out. I was too stupid to get a new, crack-free glass. This wasn't a good way to live. Down deep in my soul, I knew that. I just had to convince my brain that I needed to change.

Because I love to stir things up, I decided to finally speak to my gynecologist about how incredibly painful and awful my periods had been. Men, if you want to skip this paragraph, go ahead. But truthfully, you probably need to read this more than the ladies. My periods were awful right from the first one at age thirteen. They were always unpredictable, often deciding to begin while in school and usually when I was wearing light colored pants and was without a tampon. I always struggled with it and accepted it. In the spring of 2014, after a particularly bad period that lasted for over two weeks, I finally spoke to my gynecologist and was sent for a transvaginal ultrasound. MEN: If your woman or mom or ANY female you know has ever had a transvaginal ultrasound, you need to go out right NOW and buy them some flowers or chocolate or something sparkly. It is painful and humiliating and painful and awkward. And did I mention PAINFUL? I just want to drive that point home. The results of my ultrasound showed I had large fibroid tumors that were the root of my pain. My gynecologist suggested a hysterectomy, and I waved my hand and said, "Psssssh. No way." When my next period lasted nineteen days, I was back in her office scheduling surgery.

Surgery was simple, and while it was typically same-day surgery, due to my Crohn's medications suppressing my immune system, the surgeon felt it best to keep me overnight to monitor me a little longer. Things went well, and I had my uterus, cervix, and Fallopian tubes removed; my ovaries remained so I wouldn't be forced into menopause. I was on lots of pain medication while in the hospital and having a catheter jerked from my body was even more painful than the surgery itself.

Infection, which was chalked up to my suppressed immune system, plagued my recovery. After twelve weeks battling several issues, I finally began to feel better. It was a difficult time, and my parents and Jimmy were there for me endlessly. Oliver knew something was wrong with me during all of my recovery time and he had mercy on my soul by doing mostly good, solid poop, instead of his now-becoming-more-frequent soft poop. My body felt like a car that had been stolen and stripped of its parts, but there was a light at the end of the tunnel: NO MORE PERIODS. (Imagine that sentence with angels singing in the background.)

Looking back after my surgery, I thought about how interesting it was for me to decide on surgery due to mostly being uncomfortable. I had been living uncomfortably without a Crohn's remission for years and refused to make a change that could help me. Obviously, I knew a hysterectomy would resolve my problems gynecologically while jumping to a new Crohn's medication was a black hole of mystery. What would it take for me to make the change?

What Oliver Taught Me: It is okay to be afraid of change, and it is normal to be afraid of things in life that we haven't any control over. That shit can be scary. But we need to realize that by giving power to the things we are afraid of, there isn't even the possibility of change. We will continue to have the same fears.

Oliver adapted to his fear of our hardwood floor simply by turning around backward so he wouldn't see the spots that bugged him. He was able to navigate comfortably, and without fear between Point A. and Point B. Maybe life isn't always about facing our fears head-on, but adapting ourselves to be comfortable enough to find a way around them. That's not cowardice; that is ingenuity. That's not being afraid; that is doing what we can to soothe ourselves. However we face our fears—or get through the scary times—it's all a part of the lessons we need to learn.

chapter
TEN

Since moving back home after Hurricane Sandy, Jimmy and I decided we didn't want to live so close to the bay any longer. Much like my fear of birds and squirrels, the unpredictability of the water made my fear grow of living two streets away from it. As 2014 was coming to a close, my mom—who is a realtor—helped us list our house and we placed the "for sale" sign out front without much thought aside from wanting to sell it quickly. It was a strange mix of emotions for me since I had grown up in Silverton and always thought it would be my home. Since water mostly surrounds Silverton, I felt anxiety and worry that a storm of that size could happen again. We made mental lists of what we were looking for in a new home, and it didn't seem like we were asking for too much. We wanted a ranch with at least three bedrooms, at least one-and-a-half baths, a garage—oh, and an in-ground pool. Okay, so that seems a little bratty, but we believed wherever we ended up would be the place where we'd live out the rest of our lives. We rarely splurged on anything for ourselves (mostly because we could never afford to) and shit, if I'm going to die one day, why not do so lounging by a pool? We also wanted to be further inland. You know, away from any chances of water destroying our home again.

And so the hunt was on! Real estate websites became both my best friend and worst enemy. I hunted for houses, cursed houses that I liked that were off the market, and stalked houses we did like to make sure the "for sale" sign was still out front while waiting for a magical offer to come in on our home. The first house we went to see should have been a warning sign of things to come, but I chalked it up to just a bad pick of a house. It was a Colonial style home on a cul-de-sac in our town, only further from the water. It also had an above ground pool and a large piece of property. When we pulled up to it with my Mom (our realtor) and my Dad (our critical eye for all things workmanship-related) the house didn't look anything like the picture that had been posted online. Whoever took the photos of the house had to have been a Photoshop guru because they made a garbage dump look majestic.

Walking up the driveway, I instantly smelled something awful. Jimmy and my parents rolled their eyes at me. Sure, there are times when I am dramatic, but my nose knows, and boy, did it know something was wrong with this house. At the front door, while my Mom was using the lock box to gain entry, it was easy to see the front door was barely holding on by its hinges. And again, the smell was even stronger closer to the house. As soon as we stepped inside, I immediately said, "I want to leave." Everyone looked at me like I was nuts, but I have a sixth sense about things, and I felt it deep in my soul. The "animal" smell in the house was overpowering. I'm not so dumb that I don't understand animal smells. Oliver had always been a stinky dog. It doesn't matter how clean your house is; dogs and cats and ferrets and any other pet will leave a stink in your house. You just become immune to it. I smelled ANIMALS. In all caps. ANIMALS. I'm not dramatic—this was clearly a house of many animals. (I firmly believe my keen sense of smell is compensation for my horrible eyesight.) Clearly, I was the only one who thought that since everyone else was rolling their eyes at my protests of exploring this house.

The kitchen and bedrooms were located upstairs, so we went there first, and it was a pigsty. Awful, dirty, broken down, peeling paint—yet the pictures online reflected none of that. Online, the house was a dream. In-person, it was a motherfucking nightmare. As we walked through the house, I made sure not to touch a single thing. I was confident I would get Legionnaires disease if I did. After seeing the kitchen, I refused to look at the bedrooms. We walked downstairs and out into the backyard. There were animal pens set up without any animals in them, which was confusing. Did pigs live there? Dogs? Crocodiles? There wasn't any way to distinguish. We had seen enough outside and walked back into the house to make our way to the final pit stop—the garage.

At the back of the garage was a door that was slightly ajar with a light shining brightly through it. The smell in the garage was something I could never accurately describe. It reeked of animals and garbage. Or animals in garbage. Or animals who ate garbage. My Dad and I walked back to the door, drawn to it, curious as to what was inside. It was as though we were in a horror movie and we couldn't control ourselves. And, if we were in a horror film, this would be the point where whoever was sitting on their couch watching would scream, "DO NOT GO IN THERE!" We went in.

There were cages upon cages upon cages of birds. A lot of birds. The animal of which I am most petrified. They all began squawking and flapping, and I bolted. If the door to get outside had been closed, there would have been a Sherri-shaped hole in it from the sheer force and speed in which I would have run through it. I shuddered and shook the entire way home, disappointed in our very first adventure viewing a house. Apparently, these people were bird breeders—something we found out through their realtor after leaving the house. Coming home to our clean, non-bird infested home made me wonder if this was just one random bad experience, or if something was telling us not to move.

Well, it wasn't just one bad experience. We saw houses that were falling apart despite the owners wanting top dollar. We saw a house with a giant BUBBLE—which no one could explain—protruding from a wall. And when I say, "bubble" I do not mean some tiny little bubble or ripple in the wallpaper. It was a massive bubble—about a foot in diameter—that the homeowners slapped some wallpaper over. We saw two houses that claimed to have pools. One didn't have a pool, and one had a kid's inflatable pool they were trying to pass as an actual pool. It was exhausting and frustrating. Still, we knew we were in a weird predicament only because we couldn't afford to buy a house until our house sold. We looked at these viewings as "weeding out what we didn't want."

Given that just about everything was new in *our* house after the hurricane, I expected the first person who came to see it would look around approvingly. Then they would faint because of how cute, clean, and adorable it was, and then show up the next day with a giant sack of money and say, "HERE IS A SACK OF MONEY! GIVE US YOUR HOUSE!" Apparently, real estate doesn't work that way. Putting your house up for sale when homes are being elevated all around your neighborhood due to hurricane damage isn't the smartest selling tactic. We knew many people would be scared away from our neighborhood, but for my sanity's sake, we wanted to move as soon as possible.

After many awful viewings, we found a house we loved that covered every single thing we wanted in a house. Still, we could not get an offer on our house, despite many, many showings. We kept lowering the price of our house all while driving by daily the house we hoped to purchase, dreaming of lounging by the in-ground pool in the summer time. Unfortunately, and despite begging the universe every day, someone bought the house we loved. Finding out someone bought it crushed us. It crushed Jimmy more than me, mostly because he already had a man cave mapped out in the house's finished basement. I was disappointed but not so much because that house sold; I was devastated our home hadn't received any offers. I had taken such pride in our rebuild after the hurricane; I thought it would sell. I began to take the lack of offers on our home personally. Seriously, WTF? Our house was adorable.

Showing after showing on our house caused nothing but stress. Each time we received a phone call about a showing, I would run around the house doing some last-minute cleaning while spraying Febreeze so the house wouldn't smell like Oliver farts. Since most of these showings occurred while Jimmy was at work, it was up to me to lure Oliver to the car and take him somewhere while realtors showed our home to people. Moving Oliver the moose was the equivalent of having a full-time job. Each time I would say, "Come on, Oliver! We have to go!" I was met with an icy cold stare, sometimes with some stink eye thrown in for good measure. If he was napping, that presented an even more difficult challenge. After the first few showings where luring Oliver out to the car with treats did the trick, he simply didn't care to move anymore. He was bored with car rides to nowhere or trips to the park at odd times when none of his friends were there. The displeasure on his face when he saw me holding his harness, while I was breaking out into a cold flop-sweat because I knew it was going to be a chore to get him to move, was something I will never forget. He disliked me very much in those moments, even when I had a fistful of treats in my hand.

There were times when I would put his harness on him while he was still lying down. I would then have to put my hands under his belly and force him to stand up so that I could buckle the harness. Then, I knew I had to act fast. If everything wasn't ready—keys in the door, car door open, treats in hand—I risked him lying back down. There were many times when I would literally slide Oliver on his ass across the hardwood floors to the front door. It was common for us to back out of our driveway as the realtors and prospective buyers were pulling into the driveway. I would silently say a prayer that I wouldn't shit my pants since I wouldn't be near a bathroom for an undetermined amount of time—and that I would be able to get Oliver out of the car when we returned home. (Once he was comfortable in the backseat, he didn't have any interest in moving again.) These showings were extremely stressful for me and annoyingly unpleasant for The Prince of Silverton.

And despite many, many, many showings, and many months on the market, and MANY price reductions, we consistently heard the same feedback: everyone loved our home, but no one wanted to buy a house where they would then have to pay flood insurance. This was so frustrating, mostly because I GOT IT. *I* didn't want to pay fucking flood insurance anymore, either! Why the hell else would I want to go through the stress of trying to sell and buy at the same time? Who could blame anyone for not wanting to buy this house? This cute, new-from-the-sub-flooring-up-because-of-the-hurricane   house. Flood insurance is expensive! We rode wave after wave of being hopeful with each showing and each realtor saying their buyers might be interested, to then feeling defeated when those two shitty words— FLOOD INSURANCE—were brought up. Unfortunately, there was a similar ranch, not even a half of a mile down the street from us that was also for sale, and they had an in-ground pool. Anytime someone would come to view our house I was sure they were going to see that other, not-as-cute house also. Each time that house dropped their price even a smidgeon, I would call my Mom in a panic, and we would lower our price to always just a few bucks under their price. If one of these ranches were going to sell, then BY THE POWER OF ALL THAT IS HOLY AND GODLY AND WHATEVER, it would be OUR house.

In between the stress—even though I reminded myself that things happen the way they are supposed to happen—I took advice from EVERYONE. Because a Catholic friend told me to, I planted a St. Joseph statue upside down near the "for sale" sign and to increase our odds, every day I said a prayer called "To Sell A House" that I got off of the internet. I panicked when I read contradictory things about where I should have placed the St. Joseph statue and more than once, made Jimmy dig it up so we could move it. If someone had told me to plant a Cabbage Patch doll while standing on my head singing "The Star-Spangled Banner," I would have done it. I downloaded many prayers and mantras to repeat every day. I prayed. I mantra'd. I wrote the address of one of the houses we loved over and over again in a notebook, believing if I put it on paper, I could make it happen.

I then brought out the heavy artillery, and I created a vision board after reading the book, *The Secret*. You cut out, draw, and write what it is you want, smack it all onto a big poster board of some sort and focus on it every day, visually. The main points of *The Secret* are, "Ask, Believe, and Receive!" You **Ask** the universe for the things you want. You **Believe** in the universe hearing you and you **Receive** what you have sent out to the universe—while using your vision board to help you, well, envision it. Ask! Believe! Receive! I'm not crafty enough to make an actual vision board, so I downloaded an app to my phone and created one there, hoping the universe would forgive my lack of being able to be crafty. I put a picture of a ranch with a pool alongside a sack of money. I worried the universe might not have access to my phone but then thought, DUH, as long as I am putting it "out there" then my delivery shouldn't matter, right? Besides, it's the universe; it knows everything. Right? And so I Asked! I Believed! I even Begged a little, just for good measure. Then I waited to Receive. And waited. And waited.

We started making excuses for why our house wasn't selling and with that came more price reductions. First, we decided we put it on the market at the wrong time of the year. If a small (and I mean SMALL) family were to buy this home, their kids would currently be in school. Logically, not many families are going to make a move during the school year. BAM, excuse number one—price reduction!

The house next door to us, or the cesspool as we usually called it, had been vacant for a year, in foreclosure, and looked like a war zone. The people who lived there were the vilest human beings who made our lives hell. When they went through a divorce and the wife moved out, the husband stayed as long as he could without paying the mortgage. When he ran out of time, being the solid human being he is, he notified all of his scumbag friends that they could take whatever they wanted from the house. The house was completely stripped clean from appliances to the kitchen sink to the water heater. Oh, and the front door. They took the *front door*. The property maintenance company hired by the bank came and instead of replacing the door with, you know, an actual door, they used a giant piece of plywood with a padlock and spray-painted the address on it. So, with each showing we had on our cute, newly renovated house, prospective buyers would see this stupid eyesore without a front door, assume it was in the state it was because of Hurricane Sandy and it would scare them away. BAM, excuse number two—price reduction!

With each of these realizations, and with a neighborhood still largely under construction from the hurricane, we kept lowering our price. My heart broke each time we shaved more off of the price— not because of potential profit we were losing, but because of all of the *literal* blood, sweat, and tears that went into turning a pile of hurricane rubble into a home again. I felt so desperate to leave this house solely based on the remote chance of another hurricane *possibly* happening sometime in our lifetime again. It was all very unsettling.

Part of me knew I was going about this all wrong. Getting what we want in life isn't that easy. And, I know that deep down inside. I figured it couldn't hurt to try every single thing in the world that might help us get what we want. I truly had to remind myself that we can't force things to BE what we want; they will BE what they are supposed to BE. I practiced a mindset of letting things naturally happen. Sure, feeling shitty due to Crohn's and trying to keep the house spotless for showings, while dragging a semi-fat bulldog out of the house multiple times per day so strangers could walk around and critique our house was exhausting. But it was a necessary part of the end game of selling our house and moving. It had to be this way. There wasn't a magic wand to wave and POOF; we'd have everything we'd want. It was just how it had to be, and so it was.

So the showings continued, and Oliver still was his usual curmudgeon self and refused to make this any easier on me. I mean, fuck, I couldn't blame him. The dude was displaced for quite a while and had to get used to new surroundings in his temporary home. Then he finally moves back home to all new belongings and scary wood floors. I learned quickly that for all of these showings of our house, it was easier to (literally) slide Oliver across the floors to the front door. Then I would lure him into the car with LOTS of treats and then drive around our neighborhood, passing by our house every few minutes to see if the showing was over. Physically getting Oliver in and out of the car at the park, especially during the winter months when he refused to let his precious paws touch snow, was too much work for both of us. Of course, it was much easier as Oliver had been losing weight on his new diet for the previous eight months. Our chubby guy was now down to fifty-nine pounds, and he looked fantastic. Still, he only moved when he felt like moving, and it could sometimes take me up to twenty minutes to get him back out of the car when the showing was over.

There were many times when I would stare at him not believing this was the same dog who was a complete terror as a puppy. Now he was just a pile of Oliver. He was too comfortable lying down in the backseat of the car as I drove him around the neighborhood waiting for random people to leave our house. He would glare at me while I stood freezing in the cold, begging him to get out of the car—all his treats consumed by that point. If looks could kill, Oliver would have murdered me a million times over during these episodes. It was my punishment for interrupting his naps each day. Murderous stare-downs from my bulldog was my cross to bear.

It was when 2014 transitioned into 2015 that my best infusion buddy, Patsy, moved back into his home since the hurricane and returned to the hospital for infusions. The "Frick and Frack" of the hospital were back together! We resumed our time together during treatment right where we left off, mostly because we had stayed in contact throughout our time apart. As if being out of his home due to the hurricane wasn't enough, in that time Patsy and his wife had been through so much. Illnesses, hospital stays, and surgeries plagued them. Each time Patsy and I spoke on the phone, or during the times I would go to visit him when he had been in the hospital, my heart felt like it was breaking. They just wanted to be back in their home. It was that simple. Patsy looked tired when I would visit him, and he began to speak differently. There was more than one time when Patsy would comment, "I don't know how much longer I can take this." I did my best to do what we always did for each other: listen.

Despite having a very extensive surgery on his nose for skin cancer and while living in constant pain, Patsy seemed in much better spirits once he returned to "our" hospital. Everyone knew him there, and everyone had missed him so much. During our first infusion back together, I surprised him with a new baseball hat I had made with the logo for his Navy Destroyer after he had lost his in the hurricane. That had been his signature hat, and nothing seemed right without seeing it on his head. He was genuinely so happy and thankful I had done that for him, and seeing him slap it onto his head and smile made everything seem somewhat normal again. Well, as normal as it could be for two people hooked up to IVs for hours on end.

We resumed our early morning arrivals for treatment, and we would sit in the waiting area, chatting away. Things were different; Patsy was now coming to treatment in a wheelchair, and he had lost a significant amount of weight. He joked with me that I wouldn't be able to recognize him since he had reconstructive surgery on his nose but honestly, the amount of weight he had lost and his frailty was more troublesome. Through all of these years, if I had learned one thing about Patsy it was that he was resilient. I knew being back in his newly rebuilt home, back at his familiar hospital for treatment, and resuming some normalcy again in his life would boost his spirits. We laughed so much during our infusions and phone calls. I would tell him stories about looking for houses and about trying to sell our house. I would tell him all about Oliver's antics, and he got such a kick out of it. Having my hospital friend back meant the world to me, too. Now with the hurricane behind us, we felt as though we had won a war—Patsy's war much more treacherous than mine. We commiserated, we laughed, and we made the best of it all. Some people might think it's weird for me to say that the hospital and my treatment times were fun but they were—all because of Patsy. We understood each other. At least in one area of my life, things felt comfortable again.

Because having a house for sale while trying to find a house to buy wasn't stressful enough, Oliver decided in January of 2015 to up the ante by getting sick. One night, at three a.m., Oliver woke up and went to the back door. Oliver typically didn't go to the bathroom in the middle of the night, but hey, when you have to go, you have to go. And he had to go. He began doing diarrhea, and at first, we weren't too concerned. Shit happens. Literally. And sometimes it takes the form of diarrhea. Take it from the chick with Crohn's disease, I can relate. That night was rough with many episodes of diarrhea. Naturally, I called and made an appointment with Dr. Denyer first thing in the morning to have him checked out.

Of course, as soon as we arrived at the vet the next day, you'd never know that Oliver was sick all night. He was so excited to be there and so happy to see some of his favorite people like the receptionist Faith Gargan, and Rachel Corvasce, a vet tech—and most especially, Dr. Denyer. Despite going there often for weigh-ins and small issues over the last year, Oliver treated each visit as if he hadn't seen them in years and certainly believed they were all gathered there, waiting for him to arrive. To Oliver, Small Animal Veterinary Associates was not a veterinary office; it was a place where a bunch of people stood around, waiting for him to visit so they could shower him with attention. I believe he really thought that! Faith's job wasn't just to answer phones and make appointments (and the millions of other things she does). Oliver must have thought she happened to do those things to kill time until he visited again. In Oliver's mind, Faith's existence on the planet was to hug him, scratch him, and shower him with attention. And, to Faith's credit, she always did. They had a special bond. I only had to say her name and Oliver would run from the car right into the office without hesitation.

That day, Dr. Denyer did an examination and checked Oliver for dehydration, and he was okay. We were sent home with some medication to stop diarrhea and told to feed him a bland diet of boiled chicken and rice for a few days. Oliver was never given "people food" before, aside from small pieces of cheese now and then if we needed to hide pills or tablets of any kind. When he had those first few bites of chicken and rice, his eyes widened, and he began inhaling his food like a wolf. I had to physically pull him away from his bowl, make him pause, rest, and breathe.

Despite being on Metronidazole for diarrhea and a bland chicken and rice diet, Oliver's diarrhea continued over the next few days. Dr. Denyer kept in constant touch with us, and she continued to make sure Oliver was hydrated, as well as giving us different medications to try when each drug failed to get his diarrhea under control. He would have a normal bowel movement here and there, with diarrhea in between. It was perplexing. A few days later, Oliver ran outside and started doing diarrhea, unlike anything I had ever seen before. It was as if someone had hooked up a hose to his ass and put the pressure on full blast. I felt awful for him, and as I watched him walking in circles, turning our backyard into a chocolate river that rivaled Willy Wonka's, I noticed swelling in his hind legs. This scared me. It was a Saturday afternoon, and I said some prayers while calling the vet's office, hoping they would still be there. Despite having just closed and Dr. Denyer being off for the day, we were told to rush Oliver right over, and another vet would see him.

After an exam with the wonderful Dr. Calabro, he determined that due to diarrhea, Oliver's hind legs were filling with fluid, which is known as edema. He was given an injection to stop diarrhea, given subcutaneous fluids (which looked like a camel's hump under his fur on his back), we were told to continue his bland chicken and rice diet, and given some more new medicine to try. Thankfully, Oliver's diarrhea stopped, and by the next morning, Oliver's legs were normal again. Poor Oliver had worked so hard to lose weight for over a year; the last thing he needed was fat legs!

A few days went by, and Oliver was doing well, all while still scarfing down boiled chicken and rice. And then, the shit hit the fan again. Rather, the shit hit the backyard again. Oliver's diarrhea was back, and while, thankfully, he didn't fill with fluid in his legs, clearly something was wrong. All of the medications he had been on for almost two weeks and a bland diet were not helping. At best, the drugs would work for twenty-four to forty-eight hours and then diarrhea would begin again. Dr. Denyer had us bring Oliver in again and ordered full blood work. When the results came in, we were all startled. Oliver's Total Protein level was extremely low, as was his Albumin. Apparently, this diarrhea was taking a toll on our sweet boy. And for as sick as he was, you would have never known it by how happy he was each time he arrived at the vet's office. He still wiggled as if his body just couldn't contain his excitement. If anything in life is getting you down, think about this: Oliver was so sick, he felt miserable, his blood work was a mess—yet that sweet boy never once did anything less than give love to every person in his path.

I am very much like a bulldog in that I am stubborn. I cannot let things rest until I fully understand them. I need to know how things work, why things are the way they are, and how to fix anything broken. With Oliver's blood work results being so awful, I began Googling the shit out of each component of his blood work so I could understand each part of it—something I never even did for my own blood work. The numbers from Oliver's Total Protein and Albumin were alarmingly low. Scary low. Like, how-is-this-guy-even-functioning, low. Dr. Denyer felt sure that Oliver was experiencing Irritable Bowel Syndrome and I agreed. The symptoms were there, and the signs in the form of his blood work results were there also. I would stay up at night researching and comparing Oliver's Irritable Bowel to my Crohn's. We used to joke about Oliver mirroring me and vice versa. From injured legs to styes on our eyes, we connected more and more on a strange level, medically. This instance wasn't any different. I wished he didn't have to experience anything like I have to with Crohn's. While Irritable Bowel is different from Crohn's, each has their triggers for symptoms. I knew I had to look deeper into his illness and his diet seemed to be the best place to start.

Here is the thing about Crohn's that not many people understand: Crohn's disease is an autoimmune disease. Food does not play a clear role in curing Crohn's. It can help inflammation or cause inflammation, but diet will never cause or cure Crohn's. There isn't a cure for autoimmune diseases. As a Crohnie, I know which foods I need to avoid, and those are anything high in fiber and mostly all raw veggies or fruits with skins, which are difficult for me to digest. So, having that knowledge, I began to look at Oliver's diet back when the Irritable Bowel started (while he was on his prescription diet food) and the food that he was eating while in the throes of Irritable Bowel (boiled chicken and white rice). The common denominator between the two was chicken. Could Oliver not be getting better and his diarrhea becoming worse because of a chicken intolerance? When dogs suffer from gastrointestinal issues, the usual "go to" is a bland diet of boiled chicken and white rice. It is the first logical step towards stopping gastrointestinal problems in dogs. Since making that change to chicken and rice, he wasn't any better at all, aside from brief reprieves medication would give him. It had to be the *chicken*! After presenting my connection to Dr. Denyer, she agreed it could be possible, and so a food change was the next step.

Over the span of a few weeks, Oliver tried a few new foods. Typically, when changing a dog's food, it is done slowly over time, so as to prevent stomach distress to new ingredients. Because Oliver needed a resolution quickly and because he had only been consuming chicken and rice, we were given the okay to test a new food at a quicker pace than normal. And when that didn't work, we tested another. And when he was still shooting diarrhea, painting our backyard in shit, we tried another. These changes in food took a long time to do, yet nothing was helping Oliver, and his blood work continued to reflect how sick he was. After trying unsuccessfully to rule out food issues, Dr. Denyer felt we should take Oliver to a nearby veterinary hospital to meet with an internist. This was the same hospital where he had his knee surgery done, and despite the successful surgery, we were less than happy with the doctors and surgeons there. Still, Oliver needed help, so we went there.

I am someone who used to doubt herself endlessly. Over time, I have learned to trust my gut instinct. It's usually right. We met with an internist, and from the second he entered the examining room, I disliked him. He didn't even look at Oliver. It was the equivalent of a human going to a doctor who refused to make eye contact with their patient. It felt wrong. This veterinarian could have been the best internist in the world; if he wasn't going to engage Oliver or show any compassion or kindness, it wasn't going to be right. He examined Oliver and told us Oliver needed to have an endoscopy done the next morning so he could take biopsies of Oliver's intestines. He felt Oliver had Protein Losing Enteropathy. When I asked what that was, he didn't give me an answer. He said, "Let's take the biopsies first." We left there feeling overwhelmed and confused and very much as though the internist was rushing us into a procedure that, frankly, worried me. Oliver wasn't a puppy anymore, and bulldogs don't always do well going under anesthesia. Still, as we paid our unbelievably high bill, we made an appointment for the endoscopy for the very next morning.

As soon as we got into the car, I began crying uncontrollably. We sat in the parking lot, and Jimmy just stared at me as if I had six heads. He asked what was wrong and I explained it as best as I could. I told him I believed in my gut, Oliver should not have this procedure. I felt he would die during it. I was scared and petrified, and aside from that, it was hard to explain. I knew—*I KNEW*—this was not the right procedure at this time. I told Jimmy that I needed to call Dr. Denyer immediately and discuss it with her.

Through Winnie's life, and even more so Oliver's life, Dr. Denyer became someone who I trusted implicitly. She never once spoke about anything related to either Winnie or Oliver without thoroughly explaining herself. Dr. Denyer was so intelligent, kind, and compassionate—not just with our dogs, but with us, as well. I knew that I could explain my gut feelings about this endoscopy to her and she would know where I was coming from without ever thinking I was weird. (Well, I'm pretty sure she knows I'm weird—but in a good way, not a scary way.) Dr. Denyer has always been someone whom I connected with on a higher level than just a typical veterinarian/client relationship. We understand each other on a deeper and almost spiritual level, and throughout Oliver's time under her care, we often had discussions that extended beyond the veterinarian world. I do believe I am empathetic and especially with Oliver; I would take on every single malady he had, often feeling it myself in a way that isn't quite physical, but rather emotionally and spiritually. Maybe that was why we mirrored each other so often— because I took on whatever illness he was experiencing. I felt for certain while this endoscopy might be a procedure for the future, in my gut it wasn't the procedure for this moment in time.

I called Dr. Denyer on our ride home, and we spoke. I explained what the internist wanted to do and I described how I felt. The best feeling in the world is having someone you respect agree you made the right decision. She felt Oliver was too ill to go under anesthesia also and wholeheartedly agreed he shouldn't until he was stable. She then told us she would love for another internist at another veterinary hospital to see Oliver. Fortunately, this was an internist we had seen before with Winnie, and we felt comfortable going to her. As soon as we arrived home, I called and canceled Oliver's endoscopy. I knew we would eventually get to the root of his illness, but he wasn't going under anesthesia until we were one hundred percent sure he was stable enough to handle it.

Trying to sell our house, trying to find a house to buy, my Crohn's disease and Oliver's Irritable Bowel were all making sanity escape from my being like steam from a teapot. There was only so much stress I could handle, and I felt as though I was never quite sure which stressor needed the most attention. I realized that Oliver needed the most attention. After all, he was our fur kid. He needed our help, and we needed answers as to how to make him feel better. I hoped with the knowledge I had of my Crohn's disease I could save Oliver from experiencing more sickness. I began researching Protein Losing Enteropathy in dogs since the internist didn't offer us any information. The things I read frightened me, but I also didn't want to assume the worst. With each day that went by, I would remind myself to take some deep breaths and to focus on what—or who—needed me most: Oliver.

What Oliver Taught Me: Go with your gut! Our bodies, minds, and spirits are in tune with what we need so don't doubt yourself. Don't be afraid to ask questions, get answers, and be the squeaky wheel until you feel settled deep inside. It is okay to question someone who is in a position to help us. There isn't anything wrong with getting the answers we need, whether from a veterinarian or a doctor. No one, NO ONE, especially someone who is there to help us, should make us feel beneath them, unintelligent, or bothersome. We are our best advocates, and we are the voices for our fur kids.

During this time I also learned to make time for the people you care about and love, whether it is family or a good friend, like Patsy. We never know what someone is dealing with in their lives and a simple conversation can make a big difference in someone's day. Appreciate the moments when you can make someone forget about the realities that might weigh them down. Make someone smile and walk away from them knowing you gave them even the smallest amount of joy.

chapter ELEVEN

The fresh feeling at the end of spring 2015 didn't last very long. Usually, when summer kicks off, I feel refreshed and full of optimism. With our house still not selling, with us at a standstill on our hunt for a new home, and with Oliver's health issues still a concern, nothing felt right. I felt off-kilter, and the stress was abundant. I'm not sure if it is because I am empathic or because I have a weird sense about things, but anxiety filled me. There was a dread inside me, and I could never quite pinpoint why. I didn't want to live in a negative state of mind, but nothing felt like it was working out the way I expected it to and the frustration of that was, well, frustrating.

During this time, Patsy began a pattern of going in and out of the hospital, and each time we spoke I would ask when I could visit him. I had always done so in the past, but his answer was always the same now; he didn't want me to visit him. While this wasn't the sickest he had been, he wasn't getting any better— only progressively worse. With one issue after the next, it seemed as if Patsy's pain was growing exponentially. In June 2015, Patsy ended up back in the hospital, and it looked as though his stay was going to be long-term. He still refused to let me visit. I didn't understand why. During one conversation he told me, "I don't think I am going to be around much longer." I knew he believed that. I waited a few days before calling him again and explained I wanted to see him. "Please don't come. I don't want you to see me like this," were his exact words to me. When he said that, an understanding came over me. And, I respected his wish. We both ended that phone call in tears, and thankfully, I said everything I wanted to say to him. To this day, I don't think anyone in his family or anyone in my life truly knows how much he meant to me, and I'd like to believe I was the friend he needed, also. I told Patsy that he made the last nine years of infusions easy for me. I said he was a fantastic friend and I told him I loved him. He ended our call by saying, "It makes me feel so good knowing I helped make your treatments easier. I love you, too."

A few days after that phone call, on July 2, 2015, Patsy passed away.

His death broke my heart. It crushed me. Not because it was sudden, or unexpected, but because I honestly believe this was a friendship like no other: it was pure and natural and straightforward. We didn't require anything from each other except for genuine friendship. I went to Patsy's wake and met some of his family. I sat with his wife for a while, and as I was leaving, I realized the hat I gave him to replace the one he lost in the hurricane was in his casket. Whether he was buried with it or not, I don't know; but it gave me peace to see it there up by his shoulder.

The day after Patsy died, I asked him to send me a sign. I was grieving the loss of my friend and also mourning the loss of a powerful connection I had with this lovely human being. I wanted to believe that even if he was physically gone from this world, he was still around me spiritually and could hear me. I was standing in our backyard, and a dragonfly flew immediately up to my face. It hovered in front of me, literally inches from my nose. And, it made eye contact with me. I know, I know. You are reading this thinking that in my grief, I had lost my mind. Trust me when I say I am petrified of bugs. (And birds and squirrels and just about every other animal that is sketchy and weird.) When this dragonfly hovered in front of my face, I was calm. I didn't scream, as would be my normal reaction. I had asked for a sign, and I knew with my entire heart and soul, this dragonfly was my sign. I believe that, and no one will ever change my mind. And now, each time I see a dragonfly, whether real or on paper, or a symbol somewhere, I accept it as a gift—a "hello" from Patsy.

I still cry when I think of Patsy, and I tend to get emotional particularly in the hospital for my infusions. Seeing the chair he would usually sit in now either empty—or with someone else sitting in it—hurts my heart because I miss my friend so, so much. It doesn't matter how much time is passing. The funny thing about time is that it doesn't stop. Life kept moving without the physical presence of Patsy. I only know I have never had such a real friendship and don't know that it will ever happen again. I think it is a rare thing and I am thankful I experienced it. I missed him so much. I still do. Sometimes, I realize that I have it all wrong. I should feel nothing but elation that he is pain-free. I am so happy for him. I am forever grateful to that wonderful man for always listening and being such a great friend. Every night before bed, I touch the prayer card from his funeral and say, "I miss you, Patsy." I hope he can hear me.

In the midst of mourning for Patsy, we received news a few weeks later that Oliver's sister, Henrietta, passed away. Laura and the Alvarez family were devastated. Henrietta became suddenly sick due to an infection her body could no longer fight. Her passing saddened me so much, and my heart ached for the Alvarez family. There were moments where I felt guilty that we still had Oliver and they had suffered such a devastating loss. Henrietta was only four-and-a-half years old when she died. It was much too soon for her to leave this world. I've always had a theory that families without kids treat their dogs like children, while families with kids treat their dogs as pets. This theory didn't hold true for Henrietta's family. The Alvarez family treated Henrietta as a family member. She was never just a pet to them. She was spoiled, loved, and I knew how devastated they were to lose her. Processing these two losses—Patsy and Henrietta—were difficult for me. Knowing Henrietta was gone was almost as painful for me as losing Patsy, someone whom I was close to and with whom I had immediate access. Henrietta and Oliver connected us to the Alvarez's, and I felt as though that connection might now be gone.

Everyone handles grief differently, whether it is a friend or a pet we lose. And, I was learning firsthand the grieving process isn't linear. There wasn't a right or wrong way to grieve, nor was there a timeframe when it needed to be over. There were many days after Patsy was gone when I still had a fleeting thought of, "Oh, I have to tell Patsy about that!" To this day, over a year since his passing, his phone number is still stored on my phone. It's been difficult not to call it to see if someone will answer, whether one of his family members or someone new—someone who hadn't any clue about my wonderful friend who once owned that phone number.

Patsy, like myself, would get a kick out of life when it took twists and the unexpected happened. For example, he turned on his television one day and was watching the news. There was a segment featuring a bulldog, and he said to his wife, "That looks like Sherri's dog, Oliver!" When he told me he saw a bulldog on TV and that it looked like Oliver, I explained it *was* Oliver. The news had featured him for a brief segment. Patsy thought that was so funny. So, when the time came for Jimmy and me to make a big life decision just a couple of weeks after Patsy's death, it pained me not to be able to share it with him. He would have gotten a laugh at the way life was working out for me. Or, for all I know, maybe Patsy had a hand in making this happen from his place on "the other side."

After nine months of not receiving any offers on our house, my dad stopped by one day to console me over things not happening quickly enough. He came over, visited with Oliver, and then said he needed to check something outside. He walked out into the backyard and began walking around. (And let me state right now, he is a guru when it comes to measuring things and never needs a tape measure, which is funny because if you asked me to walk six feet, I might walk twenty feet, or I might walk three feet. I didn't inherit his distance savviness.)

He walked around the backyard making little mental notes and mumbling a few things while Oliver and I watched him, wondering what the fuck he was doing. He looked at me and said, "You have plenty of room back here for an in-ground pool. Why don't you just build one here? And you have plenty of space to add a half-bath. Why not put it here?" And just like that, we had exactly the meat and potatoes of what was on my vision board: a ranch with a pool and one-and-a-half baths. The weight that lifted off of my shoulders was inexplicable. I called Jimmy at work and explained my father's ideas. He was just as elated as I was. What we needed, what we wanted, was right here. I had asked the universe to please put us where we needed to be—and that was right here, where we were. Would I be afraid of another flood or hurricane? Yes. But that could happen anywhere, at any time.

As summer of 2015 ended, we began making plans for the following year to have a pool put in. The pool construction was still many months away, so I didn't focus on the stress of having massive construction going on just yet. Instead, I let it fester in the back of my brain where my OCD waits patiently to kick into high gear. Taking down that "for sale" sign, however, brought me more relief than the amount of worrying about all we needed to do to prep for a pool. In our guts, we knew things were happening as they were supposed to happen. We still never received our pile of money that was on my vision board, but I figured the universe was still working on that. We quickly realized without that giant pile of money, adding another half bath was going to be too much for us to take on financially. Not putting in the half-bath crushed Jimmy's dreams of taking a leisurely shower while I pooped in another bathroom. Having one full bath and one human full of shit from Crohn's disease is a nightmare for the other healthy person in the house. Still, we had managed this far with just a few instances of me standing outside the bathroom door screaming for him to get out of the shower before I crapped my pants. What are a few more years?

Along with the summer months came our first appointment with our new internist at another veterinary hospital. Oliver was having up and down moments. We finally found a prescription food that helped his bowel movements change from diarrhea to soft, formed poop. Along with the steroid Prednisone, Oliver was stable, but anytime he was weaned off of Prednisone, his diarrhea would return. I have never in my life been so excited to see soft poop. Each time Oliver went outside to crap, there would be a moment of fear— what would it look like? Would it be formed? Would it squirt out like a chocolate fountain? Would I need seventy-billion baby wipes to clean diarrhea as it dripped off his ass? Some days I would start cheering with glee to see a formed poop. Other days, I'd want to cry when a disappointing torrent of diarrhea shot out of his ass. Oliver didn't seem to mind any form that his poop came out, as long as he still received a treat afterward. But, we still needed answers. We had experience with this internist before; Dr. Anderson was the internist that discovered Winnie's cancer. The day she found it was the day we let Winnie go. Our brief interactions with Dr. Anderson and NorthStar Vets in the past gave us confidence she could help us with Oliver. We knew her to be kind, compassionate, knowledgeable, and not condescending—all characteristics we needed when dealing with the unknowns of Oliver's illness.

As always, Oliver was the shining star for his appointment. Dr. Anderson used all of the information Dr. Denyer had sent her, and then also ran some more tests, including more blood work and an ultrasound. As had been the case over the last many months, Oliver's Total Protein and Albumin were extremely low. He was also now showing elevated liver enzymes, and Prednisone was most likely the cause of that. Having been on steroids myself long-term and also showing elevated liver enzymes in *my* blood work, I knew that was a valid link, but we still felt good that Dr. Anderson wanted to ultrasound his abdomen.

Thankfully, he didn't need to go under anesthesia for the ultrasound, and Dr. Anderson raved about what an excellent, sweet patient Oliver was. We were so happy when Dr. Anderson told us his liver was clear and no masses were present. She did indicate that Oliver's intestinal wall was showing enlarged loops. This is a sign of Protein Losing Enteropathy—the disease the former internist mentioned—but, this could also have been temporary inflammation due to his diarrhea bouts. When these intestinal loops are enlarged, nutrients can escape through the loops—a leaky gut, so to speak. This would explain why Oliver's Total Protein and Albumin were so low. The only true way to test for Protein Losing Enteropathy (PLE) was to put Oliver under anesthesia and take intestinal biopsies to determine if Oliver had intestinal lymphoma, which is sometimes what causes PLE. The difference between hearing these scary terms and definitions now as opposed to the former internist telling us the same thing was that Dr. Anderson agreed with Dr. Denyer: Oliver wasn't at a stable enough point to go under anesthesia. Dr. Anderson felt we should continue down the path we were on with Dr. Denyer, using a restricted diet, along with Prednisone and Metronidazole to control his diarrhea and therefore, eventually reducing the inflammation in his intestines, with the goal of eventually getting him stable enough for intestinal biopsies.

With fingers crossed, a supply of medication, a ton of baby wipes on-hand, and the agreement to do monthly blood work, we continued monitoring Oliver's poop. Dr. Anderson even had me email her pictures of Oliver's shit. That's how thorough she was and how much she genuinely cared about Oliver's well-being. Oliver and I were living similar lives just as we always had, but he was finally showing small amounts of progress where I didn't. I even considered starting to eat his prescription food also to see if it would help my Crohn's symptoms. On one of our many, many visits to Dr. Denyer, we joked about how similar Oliver's life was to mine. We were even on the same medication at some points. I made a flippant remark that I should write a book about our lives without realizing it was something I wanted to do. I believe the universe heard me at that moment—even if I wasn't acutely aware of my destiny, my purpose, at that moment.

In November of 2015, we had a surprise phone call from the pool company. Since the weather had been unseasonably warm, they had decided they could begin construction on our pool. They were going to excavate, build the pool, and then cover it until spring when they would then come back to pour the concrete and finish the pool. We were very excited, but I was also very concerned how Oliver would handle the stress of his backyard being a construction zone. I shouldn't have worried; Oliver didn't mind the giant backhoe, the noise, or the commotion. All he cared about was the workers taking a few minutes to pet him. Thankfully, the entire giant hole that was to become our pool was cordoned off with safety fencing, so as ugly as it was to look at for all of the winter months, it was safe for Oliver to be out in the backyard. Granted, he only had a small amount of space that was free, but that was just a temporary issue. Once the safety fence came down in the spring, he would have most of his private sanctuary back.

Oliver made me proud during this time. His ability to go with the flow was something I envied. Construction, inspections, needing a dry well built and pumped, flooding the street—all of it was taking a toll on me. I kept trying to visualize a hot New Jersey summer and me floating around on a raft to keep my brain in check. It helped a little, but I sure wish I could have been as cool as a cucumber, the way Oliver was through it all. He took everything in stride. That could also be because he didn't know how much having a pool put in would cost.

With the pool built and covered for the winter, I shifted my focus back to Oliver. His bowel movements were becoming a little runnier every day despite still being on two medications—ones that had been helping all along. They now seemed to be failing. Oliver and I were in the same sinking boat once again, as my medication was also failing me even more than it previously had. Oliver's monthly blood work was still horrendous with continually low Albumin, low Total Protein, and low B12. At-home weekly B12 injections solved his low B12 issue. He never flinched and only cared about the number of treats he would receive after each injection. Dr. Denyer and Dr. Anderson spoke with each other frequently to discuss Oliver. Dr. Denyer and I talked even more often. She knew how frustrated I was that we couldn't "fix" Oliver. We knew that without intestinal biopsies, for which he still wasn't stable enough, we were only just trying to manage his Protein Losing Enteropathy—because we now were all in agreement that PLE was most likely what he had since he wasn't adequately responding to any treatments. And truthfully, even if Dr. Anderson was able to perform the biopsies, PLE was a disease where all you can do anyway is manage it.

Dr. Denyer gave us so much of her time. We were visiting her weekly at this point because it seemed as though Oliver's diarrhea was more and more frequent. I would often look at him and feel his pain because we were living identical lives. It was uncanny! Dr. Denyer would often call me on her drives home from work. After her long days of taking care of sick animals, she would still give me her free time to discuss Oliver and talk about his symptoms, or to talk about anything new either of us came across while researching PLE. I was humbled not only by the level of care and concern she showed Oliver, but also the care, concern, and kindness she was showing us.

I cried on the phone with her more times than I can count and always felt slightly embarrassed by it. It never mattered; Dr. Denyer was there for me, Jimmy, and Oliver...always. It was a level of genuine kindness I don't know I could ever express to someone who wasn't experiencing it. It was so deep, and all of these phone calls helped me even more than they helped Oliver. Dr. Denyer didn't know I was grieving the loss of Patsy and that that grief tied into this terrible feeling in my gut that we were losing Oliver. I never told anyone—not even Jimmy—that I felt our time with Oliver was going to be cut short. I felt it in my heart but forced myself to be positive. Sometimes, that's what we need to do just to live through each day.

What Oliver Taught Me: Things will always be how they are meant to be. It might not be how we want it to be, but there is a power higher than us that is helping us grow and learn by laying our lives out before us as they are intended. Our house didn't sell, and it was stressful on many levels, but we are where we need to be. Had we sold our house and bought a new one, we probably would have been in over our heads, financially. We think we know what is best for ourselves, but sometimes we are wrong.

If we can learn something from the pain or situations that bring us to our knees, then that pain is worth it. The pain of losing Patsy was so deep, yet I learned through that loss that I had experienced a pure, true friendship—something that isn't easy to find or give.

When I made those flippant remarks about writing a book inspired by my life with Oliver, that was something deeply rooted inside of me that I truly wanted to do. So, why did I disguise it in a joke? I believe when we are afraid to fail, we often are afraid to try. Making a joke or being self-deprecating is often a way to gauge the reactions around us. I needed someone at that moment to validate me. Lacking self-confidence most of my life, I needed someone outside of my close friends or family to validate me. Lynne Denyer did that in that brief second, and neither of us even knew it at the time.

chapter
TWELVE

By the end of December 2015, we were in a place of limbo both where Oliver's health was concerned and also, where we were with the pool construction. The pool was built and covered, but it could not progress any further until springtime. Oliver was stable as far as his Protein Losing Enteropathy was concerned, in the sense that he wasn't consistently doing diarrhea. While he had some good days and bad days, his blood work was consistent in the sense that it was awful. His Albumin remained very low, as did his Total Protein. Managing his PLE with steroids had now added an elevation in his liver enzymes, which we continued to monitor. He was also losing weight despite upping his caloric intake. While having a giant construction zone in the backyard was frustrating and annoying, at least it was what it was; Oliver's illness was a frustrating mystery because we still didn't know what caused it, or how we could stop or control his symptoms.

Because I wasn't stressed out enough, my sweet little Oliver decided to up the ante by waking up on January 1, 2016, with two bald, itchy patches of fur—one on his neck and one by his ear. We aren't new to the bulldog rodeo, and we know that skin issues are often a problem with the breed. Winnie was half-bald for most of her life, but Oliver's skin problem seemed different. Watching Oliver scratch himself to the point of bleeding in a span of three seconds warranted another trip to see Dr. Denyer. Our visits were becoming more frequent, and I was becoming embarrassed each time I had to call for an appointment. I would cringe waiting for Faith to answer the phone. I often wondered if they were judging me by how often Oliver needed to see Dr. Denyer. I would create conversations in my head that I would imagine everyone in the vet's office was having when I called. "Oh, that was Sherri Gibbons *again*. Can you believe it? That is the fifth time this month she is bringing Oliver in for an appointment! Some people shouldn't have pets!" I would hope that wasn't happening and I realize a lot of my worry was born out of my feelings of failure. I couldn't make Oliver's PLE better, and now new problems were popping up. I was following every direction and bit of guidance all of the veterinarians were giving us; why wasn't Oliver improving on any level, much less developing more issues?

As always, Oliver walked into the waiting room at Small Animal Veterinary Associates as if he owned the joint. And to be fair, everyone there treated him as if he did own it, so I guess I couldn't blame him. Watching Oliver's little ass wiggle like crazy as he waited for his "girlfriend" Faith to come out from behind the counter was hysterical. He would do this cute little twitch that began with just his tail. As his excitement and anticipation built waiting for her, that little tail wiggle would start to build into a full-on body wiggle. He loved her so much and the love she showed him made him so comfortable for every visit.

On this particular day, there was another dog in the waiting room looking at Faith for attention. After Faith had given Oliver the attention he was craving, she walked over to pet the other dog. Oliver was not happy, and he showed Faith how jealous he was by throwing up all over her feet. She was wearing Crocs at the time. You know, those rubbery clogs that everyone claims are so comfortable? Well, they have air holes in them. So, poor Faith was treated to Oliver's warm puke swimming through her Crocs. It was incredibly embarrassing, and I was so mortified. This faux pas didn't embarrass Oliver at all; he knew Faith now clearly understood his jealousy, and she would never pet another dog in his presence again.

Dr. Denyer was thorough as always and did skin scrapings on Oliver's bald patches. Nothing turned up, which was very unusual. There weren't any mites, fleas, yeast, or bacteria—nothing. We were given some ointment to stop the itch, and Oliver also began getting twenty-five milligrams of Benadryl once or twice a day as needed. If I thought monitoring what form his shit took was a dreadful task, constantly trying to stop him from scratching was even worse. I felt horrible that he had this intense itch that he couldn't relieve, and while the Benadryl helped temporarily, something was wrong as his bald spots spread in a matter of days. Oliver was frustrated with me. Have you ever had someone stop you from scratching an itch? It has to be incredibly annoying. Our concern was he would break the skin (that's how hard he was scratching), and those skin breaks could become infected.

Over the span of just a few weeks, we tried every medication, powder, and ointment known to man and dog. Nothing was helping. We visited Dr. Denyer several times for additional scrapings, and they all turned up nothing. After some discussion, Dr. Denyer mentioned Epithelial Lymphoma, and as you probably could have predicted by now, I lost my shit. It's only a matter of seconds that the word "lymphoma" translates to "cancer" in the brain. I knew nothing about Epithelial Lymphoma, so I asked Dr. Denyer what it meant. As much as she probably didn't want to verbalize it to me, she said, "The prognosis would not be good. Many pet owners put their dogs down immediately." The way to check was to schedule puncture biopsies to be done on Oliver the following day. Dr. Denyer was able to do them herself, which always comforts me. I trust her, I know her, Oliver knows her, and I can always rely on her to answer directly any questions I might have.

Of course, I came home and turned to Google and let me tell you, the worst thing for someone who is as emotionally high strung as I am to do is to use Google to look up ANY medical condition. As I read more about Epithelial Lymphoma, I was devastated to think Oliver might have it. On the other hand, the images that Google was showing me did not match up with what Oliver's bald spots resembled. I spent that entire day and night in a black hole of Google confusion and despair, but I am someone who needs to have as much information as possible. I feel more in control that way, and that is ironic considering I wasn't able to help (control) ANY of Oliver's issues. This little medical mess of a bulldog was testing my emotional stability with these problems. And trust me, I felt the struggle every single day.

Oliver's puncture biopsies went very well. Dr. Denyer took biopsies in three locations. Oliver had stitches in those areas, which made stopping him from scratching a full-time job. The biopsies were being sent out to a dermatologist pathologist in another state, so we were now in another depth of limbo, waiting for results. In the meantime, life carried on as usual: I was Oliver's personal assistant, inspecting his shit, stopping him from scratching, and waiting on him hand and foot. Or, paw and paw.

A week later, the results were in, and it was good news and bad news. The good news was that Oliver did not have Epithelial Lymphoma! The bad news: the dermatologist pathologist wasn't even sure what he had. She believed this skin reaction was drug-induced, meaning one of the medications he needed to keep his PLE in-check was probably causing it. Since Oliver needed those drugs to keep his PLE stable, "Now what?" was the only thing that kept flashing across my brain like a neon sign. Dr. Denyer felt it was time to see a doggie dermatologist, who might be able to give us other options to treat his skin besides the ones we had already tried. If you didn't know that dermatologists for dogs existed, you would be even more shocked to know that getting an appointment with one is almost impossible. After getting the names of the three dermatologists we could travel to within New Jersey, we learned one had retired, and one didn't have any appointments available for over six months. The third dermatologist was located at a veterinary hospital we had never been to, and we were lucky to get an appointment for the same week.

The dermatologist walked into the examining room with an arrogance that I can't explain. It was exuding from his pores. He said hello, and then promptly sat on the floor with Oliver. Sweet Oliver— the bulldog who loves everyone—hid behind me with his head down, not going near this man. Jimmy and I were embarrassed, but I also knew Oliver despised this man. I could feel it and see it in Oliver's face. He wasn't afraid of him; he overtly disliked him.

The dermatologist asked me to explain why we were there. Because the dermatologist pathologist told us that Oliver's skin issues were most likely drug-induced, I started explaining why Oliver was on those drugs. The doctor cut me off and said, "I don't care about that. I am only asking about his skin." I felt that was rude, especially since Oliver's PLE and terrible blood work results could all be reasons this was happening to his skin. As I tried explaining the connection between Oliver's skin and his medications again—as per the dermatologist pathologist who analyzed Oliver's biopsies—this man cut me off mid-sentence and began addressing only Jimmy, while ignoring me. As someone with Crohn's, I know firsthand how the gut and gut-related illnesses can cause problems through all areas of the body, such as the skin and hair. Did this jerk-face not know that? If I could have given him that information by punching it in his head and not getting arrested, I would have done so. Since violence isn't the answer, I said nothing. *Literally*. I clammed the fuck up. I felt very disrespected, so I went mute. This stupid man made me regress to the mentality of a four-year-old.

I stood there, glaring at this asshole. If my eyes could have been lasers, the dermatologist would have had holes burned through his face. The dermatologist—aka Mr. Wonderful—examined Oliver's skin. He didn't do scrapings; he didn't ask about the puncture biopsies. He didn't ask about medications; he didn't ask about Oliver's food. His solution? Give him fifty milligrams of Benadryl two times per day. In other words, we would have to buy a huge shovel to move Oliver around from one place to another as even just twenty-five milligrams of Benadryl made him sleepy. Clearly, this wasn't an allergy or reaction to anything topical. The fact that I knew that and Mr. Wonderful didn't, infuriated me. We walked out, after paying our $500 bill, and I vowed never to go back nor would I ever recommend anyone go to that hospital.

I was disappointed because I had hoped a fresh pair of eyes from someone specializing in SKIN might help us. Instead, Mr. Wonderful spoke to me in a condescending manner, and I walked out with even less of a solution than when we had begun. Some people get a diagnosis—either for themselves or their kids or pets—and they don't like that diagnosis. So, they "doctor shop," looking for a doctor who might give them another diagnosis with a more appealing outcome. That wasn't us. We wanted answers. We *needed* answers. This dermatologist wasn't even giving us an ounce of compassion or anything other than arrogance. It was disappointing, frustrating, and annoying.

We returned to see Dr. Denyer the following day for more blood work, and when I recapped our dermatology visit, she was upset. Dr. Denyer had come to know us very well. She knows we are open to people, open to receiving help, and that we were trying to do everything in our power to help Oliver. I think she felt as let down as we did—as if she steered us in the wrong direction. It is my hope she never felt that way. Dr. Denyer—more than anyone else—was our biggest supporter through the ups and the downs of Oliver's medical issues. I believe she was as hopeful for answers as we were. We were back at square one, but there is no one I'd rather have been there with than Lynne Denyer.

Throughout this time, I spent not enough time taking care of myself and way too much time trying to find answers for Oliver's illnesses. I wasn't getting enough sleep, and I wasn't eating well. Those two things put stress on my body and forced my Crohn's into overdrive. At an appointment with my gastroenterologist, he told me the antibodies I had now built up previously had almost doubled, and Remicade was essentially a complete waste of time. I had to agree. In the past, I was clinging to the three or four days after each infusion when I would feel semi-human. I didn't even have that anymore. It wasn't working, and I didn't have a choice. As scary as it sounded, it was time to make a change. And so, I was put on Cimzia injections. Also an immunosuppressive drug like Remicade, I still had to go to the hospital and get pre-medicated with IV steroids and IV Benadryl. The plus side was I didn't have to stay for hours hooked to an IV. After my pre-medications, I would receive two injections, either in my stomach or my thighs, rotating each time. My doctor explained while some people experience relief within one to two weeks, it could take up to twelve weeks to take effect, so I couldn't be immediately discouraged if I didn't see results. With my fingers crossed, I finally made the change after nine years of Remicade infusions to Cimzia injections.

Spring came and finally, the pool company completed construction on our pool. Separate companies came to pour the concrete and hook up the electrical. Then, the pool was filled with water just waiting for the heat of summer to come. We were very excited! Jimmy and I never splurge on much, and we have always lived our lives buying what we needed, not what we wanted. We were happy to have food, a roof over our heads, and our boy, Oliver, so splurging on luxury items weren't a priority for us. The pool was a major bonus, a big gift to ourselves. We were both looking forward to swimming and enjoying the summer. With the pool finished, I could now put my focus where I felt it needed to be—not on myself, but on Oliver and his weird illnesses. And, I guess that was the wrong decision. The universe let me know—via a series of powerful messages—to start taking care of myself.

After reaching the regular period in which Cimzia should have helped my Crohn's disease symptoms, I made an appointment with my gastroenterologist to discuss how awful being on Cimzia was for me. Not only was it not helping my symptoms, but it seemed as if the nurses were injecting me with water instead of medication—that's how ineffective it was. The injections did absolutely nothing for me. I also began having very weird side effects. My eyelashes fell out in clumps. My nose kept bleeding. You know, because shitting a bunch of times a day wasn't enough, I was going to be eyelash-less with blood dripping out of my nose while running to the bathroom. I had more success when Remicade stopped working than I did at this point with Cimzia. I was scared, frustrated, and so tired of shitting fifty-million times a day.

Stress can cause Crohn's to flare, but it honestly seemed as if I was back at square one with Crohn's. I had recently seen a commercial for a newly approved drug for Crohn's, and while I didn't know anything about it, I was hoping it might be something to which I could switch. My doctor agreed, and so I was taken off of Cimzia injections and switched to Entyvio infusions. While my hospital time hooked to an IV was going to increase again, it was worth those extra hours since Cimzia wasn't helping at all. I was back on the high dive, ready to leap off into the unknown once again. And I hated it. I didn't know anyone who had been on Entyvio that I could compare notes with, and even the nurses at the hospital had only a patient or two on it.

After the first couple of Entyvio infusions, I did notice it was helping me more than Cimzia had. Even with all of the stress of

Oliver's illnesses and caring for him, I wasn't running to the bathroom a million times a day on Entyvio. I was down to maybe half a million. So, with a few more infusions, I was hopeful maybe we were finally going to make some progress on the Crohn's front. It's so scary not knowing what is going to help your body—or, not help it. As someone who usually prefers being in control, Crohn's disease is a living nightmare for me, especially when having to put trust in these medications that don't always help. Still, I did my best to be hopeful.

With Crohn's disease, I had grown used to it affecting other parts of my body, such as my joints. A familiar ache in my bones was simply something I had learned to live with over the years. One day, I woke up and felt as thought I couldn't move. Every bone in my body—my knees, fingers, wrists, hips, ankles, toes—felt as though they were rubbing together. I was in a lot of pain. At first, I thought maybe this was all related to not sleeping well due to stress from worrying about Oliver. That's the fucked up thing about an illness like Crohn's—I never know if I am experiencing something new due to Crohn's, or if there is something else wrong with my body. My gastroenterologist saw me for an emergency appointment and suggested this was deeper than a Crohn's issue and suggested I make an appointment with a rheumatologist. I was lucky enough to get an appointment with a rheumatologist quickly, and in June of 2016, he officially diagnosed me with Rheumatoid Arthritis. Apparently, I had won the lottery when it came to autoimmune diseases!

The rheumatologist immediately put me on Methotrexate, another immunosuppressive drug. Methotrexate, much like Remicade, is classified as a chemotherapy drug. While the dose used for non-cancer patients is significantly less, Methotrexate still causes some side effects. I was instructed to take six pills, all at once, one time per week. After the first dose, I was instantly nauseous for several days, and rather quickly, my hair started falling out. My doctor suggested I begin taking a maximum dose of folic acid to help with the hair loss. The good news was that even after just a couple of weeks of Methotrexate, my joints felt much better. My hands were still in lots of pain but the bigger joints, such as my hips and knees, felt much better. FINALLY, some hope!

After a few more weeks on Methotrexate for Arthritis and Entyvio for Crohn's, I felt a little more human. My biggest issue was that Methotrexate was making me extremely nauseous. After another visit to my rheumatologist, he suggested that I switch from the Methotrexate tablets to Methotrexate self-injections. It's logical: by swallowing the tablets, they are being broken down and causing my stomach to become nauseous. By injection, the Methotrexate will, of course, bypass my stomach; I shouldn't experience any nausea. While slightly squeamish about having to inject myself, I knew if I wouldn't feel sick for four days out of the week, it would be worth it. I was scheduled for an appointment to learn how to inject myself safely.

I was very nervous the day of my injection training, but once in my doctor's office, I felt a little better when the nurse explained how quick and easy it would be. And it was. I was taught to clean the area of my stomach, get the needle ready, pinch some of my chubbiness, and quickly inject. It was easy! I was a master at it! I felt empowered! I felt invincible! I was no longer going to have crippling nausea every week! I WAS WONDER WOMAN!

Yeah. That didn't last. In fact, whatever the opposite of Wonder Woman is, that was me.

As I pulled out of the parking lot of my doctor's office and began to drive home, I didn't have a clue that my life was about to change. The core of my being was about to be tested. I didn't know that in a matter of five minutes, a life-or-death situation was about to occur and that I would make the wrong choice—yet, somehow, still live. I didn't know that I was going to shortly change the way I think, believe, behave, and live.

As I pulled out into the traffic of Route 37 West and drove approximately fifty feet from my doctor's office, I felt weird. I know that as you read that you probably don't find it surprising, as this book as most likely given you the impression that I *am* kind of weird. This weirdness was different. It started with my eyes. They began watering in this weird way. They felt glassy and unfocused, and a quick glance in my rearview mirror confirmed that I looked as if I smoked a bong for three days straight. While that thought entered my brain and caused me to chuckle a little, I realized my laugh sounded a bit strange. It was in that second I noticed my throat was starting to close and my tongue was beginning to swell. Having experienced anaphylaxis previously during my first Remicade infusion—the incident that began my friendship with Patsy—I knew that was what I was experiencing. When it happened the first time, I was in the hospital and surrounded by nurses who knew how to handle it. This time, I was sitting in traffic in front of a fucking Wawa convenience store, caught between panic and confusion.

On one side of my small, dull brain I knew I had to call 9-1-1. The other half of my brain had a rush of thoughts, most of which did not involve calling 9-1-1. First and foremost, all I could think about was Oliver. He has PLE. He often has to do diarrhea. If I called for an ambulance, as I knew I should, no one would be home to let him out to the bathroom should he need to do diarrhea. Jimmy was at work; my parents were in Atlantic City. Oliver was also due for Benadryl, so who would give it to him if I was on life support in the hospital, as surely, that was where this was heading?

Cars behind me began honking because the traffic had started to move, but I was too busy having difficulty breathing to step on my gas pedal. I slowly inched my car forward while trying to figure out what I should do. I turned off of the highway to a lesser traveled road and did what a normal, sane person would do: I called Jimmy at work because, you know, he should be able to save me from there, right? WRONG. If you ever experience anaphylaxis, CALL 9-1-1 and not someone who is miles away from you and not in the medical profession. I am clearly NOT a reasonably sane person.

I was crying, choking, unable to swallow, yet I still called Jimmy's cell. He didn't answer. I called him again. He didn't answer again. So, then I did what a normal, sane person would do: I started driving home. Seriously, I know you are thinking, "What the fuck is wrong with this girl?" I know you're thinking it because even as I am writing this, I am thinking, "What the fuck was wrong with me?"

All I could think about besides not being able to breathe was Oliver. He needed his Benadryl. He might need to do diarrhea. I needed to get home to him. What if he's been scratching his neck, causing it to bleed? What if his belly hurts because he is holding in diarrhea? As someone with Crohn's, I didn't want him to feel the same uncomfortableness that I felt when it came to trying to hold in diarrhea. As I cried and drove and choked and had snot running down my face, all I could see in my head was Oliver with a look of disdain on his cute face, shaking his head, and tapping on his watch. Well, if he wore a watch, I'm confident that is what he would have been doing.

Jimmy called back after seeing the missed calls from me. I answered my phone and explained I was dying but was going to make sure Oliver didn't have to do diarrhea first. Truthfully, I can't remember what Jimmy even said to me, but I imagine it was something like, "WHATTHEFUCKISWRONGWITHYOUCALL PARAMEDICS." I hung up on him, so I could concentrate on driving while not breathing.

In the cup holder of my car, was an ancient bottle of water. And, I can't be one hundred percent certain, but I do believe Oliver had been drinking out of it and I forgot to throw it away. I decided he probably wouldn't mind if I tried drinking some of his old water considering I was about to die. So, I drank dirty Oliver water while trying to rip open a mint to see if the minty-ness would open up my airway. Mint in my mouth, gagging on dog water, I did the only truly logical thing: I started praying, talking to the universe, speaking to any higher power that might be tuned to my channel. "Please!

PLEASE! Let me get home to Oliver! Please, help me! Just let me get some air! Please! Help me! Please don't let Oliver have diarrhea and need to go out! Please don't let him shit in the house because then he is going to feel like he is in trouble when I know it would be my fault, not his!"

I took a longer route home only because I knew I could drive faster on roads which had less traffic and only one traffic light. I was doing eighty-five in a thirty-five mile per hour zone and in the back of my head, I envisioned passing a police officer and him giving chase. I was choking, crying, gagging, and speeding—knowing that if a cop tried to pull me over, I wouldn't stop until I reached my driveway. Some may argue that luck wasn't on my side given the fact that I thought I would probably die soon, but it was on my side given that I didn't see any cops.

As I got closer to home, I realized my tongue wasn't swelling anymore, and my weird screams for help to the universe didn't sound as garbled. There is a drugstore on the corner of my street, so I figured I could run in and grab some Benadryl, swallow it as I drove the last half of a mile home and Oliver's poop chute would still be okay. I know I looked deranged in the store, but my focus was only on one thing. I was not thinking about dying, and not thinking about gasping my last breath in a fucking parking lot. I was not thinking about having more life left to live, nor was I wondering about the afterlife. I didn't reflect on war, poverty, abuse, gun control, politics, or religion. All I thought about was Oliver.

I pulled into my driveway, choking down Benadryl, and feeling my anaphylactic symptoms already mostly gone. I parked my car, ran inside, braced myself for puddles of Oliver diarrhea, and he was asleep on his bed. I dropped down to the floor and kissed him and asked him if he needed to shit. He glared at me then resumed sleeping and snoring.

After washing the tears and dried snot off of my face, I called my doctor's office to let him know I couldn't do the Methotrexate self-injections anymore because I almost died. My doctor came on the phone and well, wasn't very happy with me for not calling paramedics. While I felt like I was dying, this entire episode, including the drive home took less than seven minutes. Once I knew Oliver was okay, I didn't think much about what had just happened. All I cared about was that Oliver didn't have to shit and how happy I was he didn't scratch his neck and make it bleed.

That afternoon, I casually updated my Facebook status with a simple, "I almost died today. What did you do?" It got seven "likes" and didn't get any comments. Jimmy and I discussed it briefly and then went on to talk about how happy we were that Oliver had a diarrhea-less day.

That night, as I tried to fall asleep, my logic finally returned and it hit me. I could have died.

I. COULD. HAVE. DIED.

I couldn't sleep all night. It took me hours after this horrible incident to realize that not only were my priorities fucked up, but that I even went so far as to joke about almost dying on Facebook and with Jimmy. This was serious. And, an equally important question was what stopped the reaction and how was I still able to function the rest of the day knowing I could have been dead? DEAD. As in, no longer breathing air.

All night I was awake thinking about life. My life. I consider myself a decent person. I mean, I laugh when people fall, but not in a mean way. More in a nervous laughter kind of way. And okay, I'll admit to being in the grocery store and putting cookies back in the wrong place when I realize I'd feel too guilty if I bought them. But, I usually do the right thing. I almost always make good choices. I have always tried to be a good child to my parents, a good spouse to my husband, a good mom to Oliver, and a good friend. I give to charities, I have volunteered. I have empathy and compassion. But, if I had died at that moment, would I have been okay with how I lived my life? And yes, I would have been okay with it but is "okay" good enough? And I realized, while awake in the middle of the night, that I could be better. I could be better than just "okay" if I would live a little differently. And to live differently, maybe I needed to learn and absorb more about the people in my life, the decisions I make, and the behaviors I show the world.

I began to think deeply about my life and while, overall, I feel like I'd most likely get into Heaven, I might have taken the easy way out of a lot of situations.

What Oliver Taught Me: While this isn't the end of this book, this is undoubtedly the point where it all began—where the light bulb brightened above my head. I had been writing my story, Oliver's story, without knowing how it would connect and become something. The moment when I reflected on almost dying was when I realized what a freak I am—a neurotic, take-the-easy-way-out freak. Almost dying opened my mind and heart to the understanding that I could have been a better human all of this time had I realized how easily we fuck things up and complicate our lives. Don't misunderstand me: life is hard and complicated and challenging, especially when there is a lesson to be learned. So, why do we add to that with our screwy emotions and reactions? Why can't we live simply and embrace life as it is meant to be, how *we* are intended to be—pure, loving, kind, and compassionate? You know, much like a dog.

When we find ourselves in situations that are uncomfortable or not what we think we can handle, we often beg or plead to some higher power to be relieved of the situation. What we don't realize is we have been put into that situation because there is something we need to learn. Unable to breathe, in the throes of anaphylaxis, rushing home so my dog wouldn't shit in the house and feel like he did something wrong, I didn't know there was a lesson happening. It wasn't until later that night I realized it. My brain is so muddled and messed up that I hadn't put any value on my life. Instead, I was worried about something ridiculous: Oliver "feeling like he did something wrong if he shit in the house." How fucked up is it that my life didn't matter to me at that moment?

My life was so entwined with my dog's life, so wrapped up in his emotions (and before you say anything, dogs most certainly do have emotions, so stop rolling your eyes) that I could have easily thrown away my life. I have a tendency to put myself last on the list of kindness and love. And I know I'm not alone. There is a fine line between being selfless and being a fucking idiot. I had been an idiot.

My life matters. My life has value. I belong right where I am, learning the lessons the universe or a higher power was placing in my path. But, I needed to learn to be uncomplicated, drama-free, strip-away-the-bullshit. By living my life more like Oliver, I am still learning. And it's amazing.

chapter
THIRTEEN

As each day grew warmer, Oliver's skin got worse than the previous day. His itchiness was out of control, often keeping us up all night. Poor Oliver couldn't get relief, and I felt like a fucking jerk that I couldn't help him. Besides needing a toupee as his baldness spread around his entire neck, Oliver looked okay—just skinny. He was down to forty-five pounds which technically was a good weight for him. Unfortunately, he had lost a lot of muscle from being on steroids long-term, so he looked terribly skinny. His diarrhea was becoming more frequent, and he was beginning to lose fur around his eyes. We made weekly visits to Dr. Denyer but were just spinning our wheels, all of us frustrated with not understanding Oliver's illnesses.

Dr. Denyer made the suggestion in July of 2016 that we take Oliver to a well-known veterinary hospital in another state. As she explained it, "They treat the zebras there!" What she meant was since it was a learning school, many residents and students might be studying what Oliver was experiencing, with both his PLE and his skin issues. Maybe someone was researching PLE or had more insight into it. They treated the odd cases—the "zebras"—and had much more people to use as resources for different diseases than the average veterinary hospital. We had only heard good things about the hospital; we hadn't looked at it as an option sooner simply because it was so far away from us. We decided this was probably our last hope of getting relief for Oliver, so the drive was going to be worth it. Besides Dr. Denyer, we had—up until that point—visited three veterinary hospitals, seen three different internists, and a dermatologist. We felt the hospital Dr. Denyer suggested might be THE ONE—the place that could give us some answers. Dr. Denyer went above and beyond what was necessary and called there herself to arrange not only an internist appointment for Oliver for the beginning of August but explained to them we were coming from quite a distance and set up a dermatology appointment for him also. There was a light that was shining at the end of the Oliver tunnel. I felt hopeful we were going to get this weirdo some help finally.

I was wrong.

Our visit to the hospital started off stressful with Oliver needing to fast for twelve hours. Oliver was not happy about that. Add that to an incredibly long car ride, and Oliver began throwing up bile due to his stomach being empty when we were still an hour away from reaching the hospital. We made stops along the way to clean up both Oliver and the car. We felt relief when we finally reached our destination.

Oliver was scheduled for an early morning appointment with the internist, followed by blood work, an ultrasound to recheck his liver and stomach, then after all of that, he was to have a dermatology consult. After waiting almost two hours for the internist, Jimmy and I were becoming antsy and aggravated. And so was Oliver. The poor guy hadn't eaten in hours, and Oliver LOVED to eat. After visiting the reception desk to find out what was going on and why they were delaying our appointment, we were finally brought to meet with someone who was assigned to take all of our information and details of why we were visiting. She spoke with us and examined Oliver briefly, explained the internist would be in to meet with us soon, and then disappeared. We waited. We waited some more. We waited even longer before Jimmy decided to navigate the confusing hallways to get back to reception and ask why we had now been waiting almost three hours since our appointment time. There wasn't an answer, but the receptionist told him the doctor we were seeing would be in shortly.

Finally, the internist arrived. We discussed Oliver and his issues. He examined Oliver and then told us to wait in the waiting area; Oliver was being taken for blood work and then for an ultrasound. He said we probably wouldn't see Oliver again for about an hour and a half, and if we wanted to, we could leave and kill some time elsewhere. And so, Jimmy and I went for a walk around the area. I was very nervous and not sure what to expect, but I was even more worried because Oliver hadn't eaten. I know that is a weird thing to worry about when there are serious medical issues going on, but I felt awful that he had thrown up from not eating, and I was sure he was confused. Knowing that all of Oliver's previous ultrasounds at NorthStar Vets only took about twenty-five minutes, I convinced Jimmy we should get back to the hospital and wait there. I thought for certain he would be done quickly.

I was wrong. *Again.* Have you noticed a theme?

After two more hours went by—now making our time at the hospital over five hours—Jimmy went back to the reception desk to ask where our dog was. The receptionist made a phone call and told us there was a delay with the ultrasound machine, and Oliver was "next in line." I don't know what kind of lines they were talking about because two more hours went by, and we still had yet to see Oliver since we had left him with the doctor earlier in the day.

Jimmy, who is always calm, mild-mannered, and civil, was about to blow a gasket. He knew that if he let me handle this, I would start punching people in their throats, and he most likely would have to bail me out of jail. He took charge, went to the reception desk—now eight hours since we first arrived—and *demanded* Oliver back. The receptionist told Jimmy that Oliver still hadn't had the ultrasound and was just finishing up with his dermatology consult. Why we weren't present for the dermatology consult is something we will never know. And why he didn't have an ultrasound in the eight hours he was there; we will also never know. To this day, it makes me insane.

The receptionist paged our internist, and we were brought back into the exam room. They brought Oliver in and tried to calm us down but frankly, we were both so furious, nothing would calm us down. The internist told us there was a lot of emergency ultrasounds that day which kept pushing Oliver's ultrasound back since he wasn't an emergency. I'm sorry, but eight hours worth of ultrasounds? C'mon! Bullshit! I'm not sure if that is what angered us or if we were irate because, for all of those hours, not one person came to speak with us and let us know what was going on with Oliver! And the poor dog hadn't eaten since the night before!

We were done with the hospital shuffling us around and not giving us answers, and we told the internist so. We wanted our bill, and we were leaving. He could email us any results for blood work or from the dermatology consult. I may or may not have used the word "fuck" a few times. I also explained that my use of the word "fuck" was in place of punches to the face, and I think that's when it clicked in this asshole's brain how upset we were. Jimmy, who is usually the voice of reason for the two of us, told the doctor off also. He then left with Oliver, bringing him outside to finally let him pee and poop, then to the car where we had a large bowl of his food and some water waiting for him. I stayed behind while the doctor went to get the Director of Outpatient Services because this guy was scared and knew he probably needed to bring in the "big guns" to soothe us.

A seemingly nice lady came in to speak to me who, in all fairness, had no fucking clue what happened and why we were upset. I explained it to her, told her I would never, ever, ever, ever recommend anyone come to their hospital, and she did what she thought was best: offered to keep Oliver overnight, free-of-charge, to have his tests done the following morning. UH, OKAY LADY. WE WILL LEAVE HIM WITH YOU, DRIVE OVER TWO HOURS HOME, THEN DRIVE TWO HOURS BACK IN THE MORNING AND ANOTHER TWO HOURS HOME AGAIN. Get the fuck out of here! I declined, went to the front desk to pay our $1,300 bill which wouldn't be covered by Oliver's insurance, and then ran to the car so that I could hug my Oliver extra hard. And I'm sure he hated it, just as he always hated my hugs, but this time he allowed it. It was as if he knew I needed the hug more than he needed it.

Oliver crashed on the car ride home and slept for a significant portion of it, which made me happy. I felt guilty because clearly, Oliver wasn't in the best of health and while our intentions to bring him all the way to another state to what people considered a top-notch hospital was out of desperation, we put him through stress without any results to show for it. I cried most of the way home out of guilt, aggravation, and sadness, knowing we probably now wouldn't have any answers. Our last ditch effort was a gigantic flop.

I didn't sleep that whole night. I couldn't. I stayed up, researching PLE by visiting the same stupid links I already had memorized. I Googled and looked at thousands of pictures of dogs with all sorts of skin problems. I researched every drug Oliver had ever been on during his life, whether it was related to PLE or not. I posted on dog forums and because both of his conditions were rare, didn't get any responses. The next day, the hospital emailed a report, and the only new information provided was from the dermatologist—whom we never saw. The dermatologist disagreed with the dermatologist pathologist who analyzed Oliver's puncture biopsy results. So, not only did we not have new information about Oliver's PLE, we essentially took a huge step backward with Oliver's skin condition.

When Dr. Denyer heard what happened during our hospital visit, she felt as badly about it as we did. We all wanted answers and solutions, and none of us knew where to go from this point. While Oliver wasn't in pain and his PLE was barely being held at bay, I know he was itchy eighty percent of the time. It was frustrating for all of us. Stopping him from scratching made me feel like I was doing the biggest injustice to him. That wasn't fair to him but what was the solution? I wasn't going to euthanize my dog because he was itchy, especially since we worked so hard to keep his PLE stable. I began to beat myself up. Why couldn't I find a solution? Why couldn't I help him? Was there something we were doing wrong? Was his PLE medication causing harm in other ways, manifesting in this skin illness? Should we stop doing something? Should we do more? I stopped sleeping because I allowed all of my frustrations of not being able to "fix" Oliver circle back around to me because I felt responsible for him. I felt as though every person who saw Oliver's skinny body and fur-less neck was silently judging me for failing. And, more importantly, I felt as if I *was* failing this sweet, weirdo. There had to be something we could do. *Something. Anything.*

What Oliver Taught Me: Our last chance for answers was at this hospital. By making that long trip, by sitting in that waiting room hoping, wishing, and praying for answers for all of those hours, we were doing our best—the best we could for Oliver. Not having it go as planned, I was forced to "let things go." Letting things go hasn't ever been easy for me. The answers for Oliver's illnesses weren't coming despite doing all I could to get them. I was learning that because I didn't get the results I wanted, I wasn't a failure. And more importantly, I wasn't failing Oliver.

We take leaps of faith when we are desperate for answers and in need of help. We have to take these chances. I needed to take chances for Oliver, and I started to realize, I needed to take chances for my own health as well. And taking a leap of faith to change my medication for Crohn's after nine years was also something I had to do—to do the best for myself. I was petrified to make this change, but I needed to do it and hoped it wouldn't fail.

Sometimes, success or failure is not in our control. To always turn every failure into a personal failure will squash your spirit. I felt personally responsible for Oliver's illnesses. While I was responsible for Oliver, I had no control over his illnesses. While I am personally responsible for myself, I am not in control whether medication will work for me. I learned I cannot possibly shoulder the responsibility for every single situation in life. Life doesn't work that way. I couldn't beat myself up for things out of my control.

I needed to be kinder to myself. We all need to be a little more compassionate with ourselves.

chapter
FOURTEEN

After our disastrous trip out-of-state to the veterinary hospital, Dr. Denyer and I decided that she would handle everything with Oliver's illnesses, just as she had been doing. Rather than send us anywhere else at this point, she decided that should she need to do any consults outside of her practice she would phone Dr. Anderson at NorthStar Vets. We loved Dr. Anderson and felt confident with Dr. Denyer pairing up with her as needed.

Oliver's skin condition became worse with him losing more hair and still having terrible itching in which nothing would stop it altogether. We went from weekly trips to see Dr. Denyer for Dexamethasone shots to quell the itching to visits every three days. Oliver was still in good spirits despite looking like a bald freak. His hair loss now spread the circumference of his neck. We developed a routine to keep scratching at bay by using Benadryl and Gold Bond Medicated Powder, along with the Dexamethasone shots.

We also purchased rolls of stockinette that is used on Lymphedema patients, to provide a slight, loose barrier between Oliver's nails and his skin. The company in which I ordered the stockinette from sent me a lovely email asking me if my cancer journey was going well and I was too mortified to reply telling them the product was for my dog's neck. Each time I ordered more, they would reach out asking me how I was doing and each time, I would reply saying I was "okay." Because, well, I technically was okay. It wasn't a lie. Unless they wanted to know how I was mentally, then yes, it was a lie because I was nearing batshit crazy status from worrying about Oliver so much.

I mostly became glued to Oliver, to prevent him from breaking his skin open, or I was glued to the computer, trying to research weird, random skin issues. We had been so excited to have our pool built; it was richly ironic that we barely were able to use it. Oliver needed constant supervision. Oddly enough, when in my presence, Oliver rarely scratched at his neck. The minute I stepped outside to enjoy our new pool, he would walk to the glass patio doors, making sure I could see him, and would then begin to scratch his neck with the strength of He-Man. Witnessing his scratching would cause me to jump out of the pool as quickly as I could, run inside with water dripping everywhere, just to stop him and apply Gold Bond Medicated Powder or give him a dose of Benadryl if he was due for one.

At night, I would stay on the computer for hours, hoping to find something that I previously missed that could help Oliver's skin and PLE. I would rearrange the words and phrases I would type into Google, only for it to lead me to the same few articles or forum posts. My gut was unsettled. I was always on the brink of a panic attack, worrying endlessly about my moonwalking weirdo. And guilt, oh, the guilt! This awful feeling of failure that I couldn't shake trapped me in a cocoon of guilt. If I couldn't help Oliver, and the many veterinarians we saw couldn't help Oliver, what did that mean? It meant I failed as a dog parent.

We bring these fur kids into our lives with the intention of giving them the best life possible. And, while Oliver had the best of everything, none of that mattered to me if I couldn't heal his physical illnesses. I was getting very little sleep and always feeling panicky and had a nervous energy that would cause my hands to shake. After a few particularly challenging days with Oliver shooting diarrhea and still itchy as fuck, we went in to see Dr. Denyer for his every-three-days Dexamethasone shot. Dr. Denyer walked into the exam room, and before she could say a word, I began crying uncontrollably. She gave me the best hug I think I've ever had in my life. She didn't give me that hug because I was crying; she gave me that hug because she could feel my pain.

Dr. Denyer and I spoke almost daily, and we were at her office every three days, so she knew what I was putting myself through trying to figure out how to help Oliver. I said one sentence to her that summed up how I felt: "I want Oliver to be healthy again so he can enjoy life before he dies." Oliver was already almost five-and-half and had spent almost a year-and-a-half dealing with PLE. During that time, his trips to the park became less frequent, and it seemed like he was losing energy rapidly, not wanting to play at home or go for a short walk. As I sobbed in the exam room, Oliver wiggled his ass all over the place, trying to make me look like a liar. He behaved normally, happily, and was thrilled to be getting attention even if it was in the form of a shot in the butt to control his itching.

As happy as Oliver was to be there, I was at a breaking point. I hadn't slept in almost three nights. I was desperately searching online every minute of the day for help, cures, holistic treatments, and pictures that will forever make up my nightmares. Dr. Denyer said, "Let me keep him for the day. He can hang out in the back, his favorite people will give him attention, and you guys can go home and relax." I felt embarrassed it had come to this, but I accepted the offer after some lame protests. As much as I loved Oliver, that six-hour break was the most beautiful gift. Jimmy and I raced home, threw on our bathing suits and floated in the pool for every minute of those six hours. And, it was the first time in years where I felt relief. I felt the tension leave my neck. The agony I felt in my stomach was gone. Oliver was in the best possible hands he could be in for the day. He was safe. It might make me a bad mom, but I didn't even think about him. I floated on my raft, enjoying the beautiful mid-August weather, soaking up the sun and not thinking about Oliver, his diarrhea, skin, baldness, or possible cures. It was the calmest I felt in about two years, and I wasn't even faking it.

When it was time to pick Oliver up from the vet's office, I realized how much I missed him. No matter how challenging and emotionally draining life with Oliver had been, not having him around for even a few hours felt strange. Maybe it was less to do with missing his physical presence and more that my brain didn't know what to think about if I wasn't thinking about Oliver and PLE and skin issues and what form his poop took. It felt like someone scooped a huge hole out of my brain with a giant melon baller, and I didn't know what else there was to think about. When they walked Oliver out of the back room, my eyes filled with tears because I really did miss the little kook for those few hours! And if Oliver missed us during those six hours, he played it cool by not wanting to leave Dr. Denyer's office. Jerk. As we left Small Animal Veterinary Associates, I took a huge breath and let it out in one long sigh, because despite how refreshed I felt after those few worry-less hours, I knew that soon I was going to be right back where I was six hours earlier.

And I was right. The small reprieve from OWS (Oliver Worry Syndrome) was a thing of the past by dinner time. Oliver never missed a beat and still bucked like a bronco when he saw his dinner going into his bowl. He had recently changed his after dinner routine from playing wildly with Jimmy in the living room to opting for an after dinner nap. And that was okay. His Total Protein and Albumin were still extremely low, so if the little dude didn't have the energy to play, we understood. He always had the energy to jump wildly into the air for food or treats, though. And while Oliver went about his days and nights the same as he had been, I returned to my freakish obsession with trying to fix him, searching for answers, not getting any answers, and then wallowing in guilt.

On a phone call with Dr. Denyer, I told her about the guilt I was experiencing, and she put it into a different perspective for me. She said, "Oliver doesn't know if you're finding results. He just knows you love him and are taking care of him." Was it really that simple? Not in *my* fucked up brain. In my brain, Oliver was ready to file emancipation papers because I wasn't "curing" him. Why am I so weird? Why do I impose human thoughts and emotions onto and into my bulldog? That's not normal at all. Is it? I mean, I don't think so. How do I undo my brain and remove the part that puts WAY more complicated shit than is necessary into every single thought?

I once had a horribly shitty job working for a very shitty telemarketing company. Thankfully, I wasn't one of the ogres who called you right at dinner time to ask you fifty thousand questions. Instead, I worked in a smaller division of the company, contained in a separate, smaller office. In the telemarketing section, there was a girl who worked there who had several disabilities. Truthfully, I'm not exactly sure what her particular job was since it was a large company and I didn't interact with her in a business-sense, but she would walk through our office a lot and often had very public arguments and difficulties interacting with coworkers. Every so often, word would trickle down to our office that she had had a meltdown and was emotional and crying. Everyone at the company included her and treated her as they would anyone else but still, there were differences in her emotional state that were obvious.

One day, she came into work with two maxi pads taped around her ankle. Apparently, she had cut herself and decided to tape the maxi pads around her ankle instead of a Band-Aid. It was awful because while no one directly laughed at her, everyone was whispering and chuckling about it behind her back. I had Band-Aids in my purse, so I pulled her aside and asked her if she wanted them. She said, "No" and looked at me as though I was Satan. She went about her day with two maxi pads taped around her ankle and I went about mine feeling guilty because I couldn't save this girl from people whispering about her and most likely, going home to tell their families and friends about it. She didn't have any problems walking around with maxi pads strapped to her leg, so why did I feel so guilty and weird about it? I felt guilty because her emotional pain (which I don't even think she had) wasn't something from which I could save her. And apparently, she didn't want to be saved from it, anyway.

And that is the best way I can explain my guilt over Oliver. I couldn't save Oliver from what he was experiencing, and I turned that inability into a flashing, neon sign in my brain that read FAILURE. That failure made me feel guilty. Oliver didn't have the capacity to understand what failure was, did he? Who the fuck knows, but in my pea-brain he did. And I felt guilty for failing. I made that girl's maxi pad bandage my business, and when I couldn't control her situation for her, I felt like a failure, and I felt guilty for failing. I couldn't manage Oliver's illnesses and save him, and I felt like a failure. And I felt guilty for failing.

What Oliver Taught Me: Oliver did not have any control over his illnesses, right? So why did I think that *I* could have control over his PLE and skin disease? Apparently, I felt I should be able to control it all, and not controlling it meant I was failing, which then led me to feel immensely guilty. None of that is logical, and I spent too much of my time trying to force it to be logical. If I could draw you a map of my brain and the emotions that guide it, it would be a puddle of arrows, question marks, and squirrels. None of it made sense no matter how much I wanted it to make sense. Oliver was in the same situation as me; we had incurable illnesses. I know I can't cure my Crohn's, so why did I feel guilty for not being able to cure Oliver's incurable illnesses?

Let's get real. Oliver wasn't comfortable, but he wasn't in pain. He still enjoyed his life. He had slowed down, sure. But he jumped with joy for all of his foods and treats, he played when he wanted to, he ran at top speed into the vet's office, he wiggled his entire body with joy, and he moonwalked with ease. Why couldn't I take a step back from wanting to control it all and simply enjoy this little curmudgeon's life and be thankful for every moment? Instead, I was plagued with guilt, just as I was when I couldn't get that girl to take the maxi pads off her ankles.

Not everyone needs to be saved by me. Seriously, who the fuck do I think I am? I can barely function and often ask myself if I'm even doing life correctly. So, how important do I think I am that I would ever believe I could control Oliver's (and the maxi pad girl's) emotions and the outcomes? All of this was out of my control. ALL OF IT. And it was making me spin into thoughts of failure and guilt.

FAILURE SHOULD NOT EQUAL GUILT. It just shouldn't. Sometimes things don't work out, and sometimes there are things we aren't meant to be in control of at all. Not being in control is one of my biggest fears. And it's scary as fuck for me to "let things be." But guess what? Oliver forced me to realize I just had to go with the flow and let it all be because there wasn't anything more I could do. I had to let it all go. And I wasn't a failure. I tried. Boy, did I try! For once, I needed to understand that because I failed to cure Oliver, I wasn't a failure. I needed to recognize and acknowledge just how much I tried. And be proud of all I learned in the process.

Where It Ends

Today is September 6, 2016.

Oliver became an angel this morning around 8:45 am. His body couldn't fight any longer, and we needed to let him be free. He had been doing okay, staying stable. But, he didn't look the same. Yesterday, I looked at Oliver then turned to Jimmy and said, "He doesn't look right." I feel, in my gut, I knew it was almost time. Oliver's time with us was ending, and I knew it. I just wasn't sure how to process that. Later that night, I was lying on the floor next to Oliver as he was relaxing on his "Big Boy" bed. I told him the same thing I once said to Winnie: "If you are done here, you need to find a way to let me know."

Early the next morning, after Jimmy left for work, Oliver began having difficulty breathing. I rushed him to Dr. Denyer. He was extremely sick and started vomiting everywhere before collapsing on the floor. I was hysterical to be at this point, and without Jimmy beside me because he couldn't leave work. I didn't know what was happening, or what to do. All I knew was that Oliver wasn't stable anymore, and it had happened within a matter of minutes.

Dr. Denyer held my arm and said to me, "What do you think you need to do?" I said, "I think it's time to let him go." So, we did.

His decline was so sudden—from being stable to the point where we were at now. I know it was Oliver's gift to me; I didn't have to decide; there wasn't any time to decide. Oliver gave me a clear sign he was done here, as painful as it was for me to recognize it, and see it with my own eyes.

Since Jimmy couldn't leave work, Dr. Denyer and her vet tech, Rachel, stayed with me through it all. They comforted me as I sobbed hysterically. I am still crying hysterically. Everyone—all of his favorite people at the vet's office—came in one-by-one to say goodbye to Oliver. All I could do was cry and thank each person who came to say goodbye for the love and care they had given Oliver. And, I kept thanking Oliver over and over for all he taught me. I kissed his head a million times as he closed his eyes and finally let go.

He left this world surrounded by some of his favorite people. It was gut-wrenching, emotional, and heartbreaking. Losing a family member, which Oliver was to us, isn't easy, but it is even more challenging when they are young. Oliver wasn't even six yet. We had hoped we would have many years left with him, even with his diagnosis of Protein Losing Enteropathy.

I know Oliver chose us to be his parents. I believe life is about synchronicity and the universe brought us together because I needed to learn so much that I was letting slip by before having Oliver join our family. What that weird, funny, sweet, cute bulldog taught me in his short time on Earth is not anything that could be summed up in this book alone.

He inspired me—along with Dr. Denyer and Jimmy—to begin this book, but more importantly, to finish it. I began writing about Oliver before knowing what this book would be about, and before knowing how it would end. Did I know we were going to lose him soon? No. I didn't have any idea things would turn out this way. But I knew in my gut, given his illnesses, his life wouldn't be as long as we had hoped. Still, I hoped he would be here when I finally published this book. I naively thought he would still be here when I finally figured out how to make this writing thing work. Grief has filled me so much that I don't even know how I will continue this book—but I will because what Oliver has taught me are lessons we all need. They might be lessons we already are aware of, but of which we need reminding.

I believe in my soul that as soon as I realized this book was my purpose in life, the universe knew it was time for Oliver to move on. Dealing with the grief is something I don't know I'm prepared for as I sit here and cry uncontrollably. I've been through this grief with Winnie, but we also had twelve-and-a-half amazing years with her. Oliver's time was short, and that adds a dimension to my grief that is complicated to explain.

This sweet, weird, beautiful bulldog brought some of the most amazing people into our lives. And they will remain in our lives. Oliver made so many people smile, and he helped us through one of the most difficult times in our lives: Hurricane Sandy. He lit up our world in some of our darkest moments. He made me smile, made me laugh, and most importantly, made me see my life and behavior and reactions for what they were and what they should be. This cute moonwalking curmudgeon showed me how to live as we were meant to live—open-minded, openhearted, with compassion and kindness, free of guilt, fear, and bullshit.

Oliver touched so many lives in his short time on Earth, and I already know he is running, playing, and having the best time ever, smiling down on us. Driving home from the vet this morning, with his harness and leash next to me on the seat of the car, I realized Oliver had left me with one final lesson.

What Oliver Taught Me: You cannot measure life by time. It doesn't matter if you are here for five years, ten years, one hundred years; we need to measure life in terms of <u>quality, not quantity</u>. We need to make every moment count, and we need to appreciate those moments. Oliver was only here for five years and ten months, but he lived a life filled with love, friends, family, smiles, and laughter. He touched the heart of every single person he came in contact with and made so many people laugh. He had the BEST QUALITY OF LIFE. My heart is aching so much right now that typing this isn't easy. But, I felt it necessary. This book is to honor those who are in my life and to honor Oliver, for helping me become a better human.

About the Author

After leaving her corporate job to focus on her health, Sherri Gibbons began a career in music journalism as owner of Revolt Music Magazine from 2004-2011. She lives in New Jersey and tries to surround herself with bulldogs as often as possible. Sherri doesn't consider herself an author; she simply had a story to tell.

Made in the USA
Middletown, DE
29 July 2017